Geraldine Jewsbury

Geraldine Jewsbury

Abigail Burnham Bloom

EER
Edward Everett Root, Publishers, Brighton, 2020.

EER
Edward Everett Root, Publishers, Co. Ltd.,
30 New Road, Brighton, Sussex, BN1 1BN, England.
Full details of our overseas agents are given on our website.
www.eerpublishing.com

edwardeverettroot@yahoo.co.uk

Abigail Burnham Bloom, *Geraldine Jewsbury*

Key Popular Women Writers series, Volume 3.

First published in Great Britain in 2020.

© Abigail Burnham Bloom 2020.

This edition © Edward Everett Root 2020.

ISBN: 978-1-912224-87-6 Paperback
ISBN: 978-1-912224-88-3 Hardback
ISBN: 978-1-912224-89-0 eBook

Abigail Burnham Bloom has asserted her right to be identified as the author of this Work in accordance with the Copyright, Designs and Patents Act 1988 as the owner of this Work.

All rights reserved. No part of this publication may be reproduced, stored in a retrieval system or transmitted in any form or by any means, electronic, mechanical, photocopying, recording or otherwise, without the prior permission of the copyright owner.

Cover designed by Pageset Limited, High Wycombe, Buckinghamsire.

Series editors:
Janine Hatter and Helena Ifill.

This innovative new series delivers original and transformative, peer reviewed, feminist research into the work of leading women writers who were widely read in their time, but who have been under-represented in the canon.

The series offers critical, historical and aesthetic contributions to current literary and theoretical work. Each volume concentrates on one writer.

The first five titles are available:

- *Geraldine Jewsbury* by Abigail Burnham Bloom.
- *Florence Marryat* by Catherine Pope.
- *Margaret Oliphant* by Valerie Sanders.
- *Mrs. Henry Wood* by Mariaconcetta Costantini.
- *Frances Trollope* by Carolyn Lambert.

These will be followed by volumes on:

- *Mary Braddon*
- *Rhoda Broughton*
- *Daphne Du Maurier*
- *Ouida*
- *Mary Shelley*
- *Marie Corelli*
- *Charlotte Riddell*
- *Edith Wharton*

We welcome suggestions for other titles.

The series volumes interrogate the ways in which women writers, their creative processes and published material can be considered feminist, and explore how recent developments in feminist theory can enrich our understanding of popular women writer's lives and literature.

The authors rethink established popular writers and their works, and rediscover and re-evaluate authors who have been largely neglected – often since their initial burst of success in their own historical period. This neglect is often due to the exclusivity and insular nature of the canon which has its roots in the Victorian critical drive to perpetuate a division between high and low culture.

In response, our definition of the "popular" is broadly interpreted to encompass women writers who were read by large sections of the public, and who wrote for the mass publishing market. The series therefore challenges this arbitrary divide, creating a new and dynamic dialogue regarding the canon's expansion by introducing readers to previously under-researched women writers who were nevertheless prolific, known and influential.

Studying the work of these authors can tell us much about women's writing, creativity and publishing practice, and about how popular fiction intervened in pressing political, social and cultural issues surrounding gender, history and women's roles in society.

This is an important and timely series that is inspired by, interrogates, and speaks to a new wave of feminism, new definitions of sex and gender, and new considerations of inter-sectionality. It also reflects growing interest in popular fiction, as well as a feminist desire to broaden and diversify the literary canon.

Ultimately the series sheds light on women writers whose work deserves greater recognition, facilitates and inspires further research, and paves the way for introducing these key women writers into the canon and modern-day studies.

The editors

DR. JANINE HATTER is an Early Career Researcher based at the University of Hull. With Nickianne Moody she has edited the volume *Fashion and Material Culture in Victorian Fiction and Periodicals,* already published by *EER.* Her research interests centre on nineteenth-century literature, art and culture, with particular emphasis on popular fiction. She has published on Mary Braddon, Bram Stoker, the theatre and identity, and Victorian women's life writing, as well as on her wider research interests of nineteenth to twenty-first century Science Fiction and the Gothic. She has also co-edited special issues for *Revenant, Supernatural Studies, Nineteenth-Century Gender Studies, Femspec* and the *Wilkie Collins Journal.* Janine is conference co-organiser for the Victorian Popular Fiction Association, and co-founded the Mary Elizabeth Braddon Association.

DR. HELENA IFILL is a Lecturer in English Studies at the University of Aberdeen where she is the Director of the Centre for the Novel. Her research focuses on the interactions between Victorian popular fiction, (pseudo)science and medicine. She is the Secretary of the Victorian Popular Fiction Association and a co-organiser of the Association's annual conference. As well as her monograph, *Creating Character: Theories of Nature and Nurture in Victorian Sensation Fiction* (2018), she has published work on Charlotte Riddell, Florence Marryat, Wilkie Collins, Bram Stoker, and Victorian mesmerism. She has also co-edited special issues for *Nineteenth-Century Gender Studies* and the *Wilkie Collins Journal.*

The author

ABIGAIL BURNHAM BLOOM teaches Victorian literature at Hunter College, City University of New York. She has published a book on film adaptations of Victorian works (*The Literary Monster on Film,* McFarland & Co., 2010), worked as managing editor of the journal *Victorian Literature and Culture,* edited several books on Victorian subjects, and written articles on Jane Austen, Jane Carlyle, Thomas Carlyle, George Eliot, Robert Louis Stevenson, and the Brontë family, as well as Geraldine Jewsbury. Her work, *Leading the Way for Victorian Women: Geraldine Jewsbury and Victorian Culture, Selections from her Letters, Short Stories, and Essays,* was published by EER in 2019.

Contents

Acknowledgements xi

A Note on the Text / List of Abbreviations xiii

Introduction. Rediscovering Geraldine Jewsbury. 1

Chapter 1. Early Influences: Becoming Geraldine Jewsbury . . 19

Chapter 2. The Carlyles and *Zoe*: Discovering the World. 43

Chapter 3. Fiction and Short Pieces: Educating Readers 61

Chapter 4. Letters: Jane Welsh Carlyle, Walter Mantell, and Other Friendships. 85

Chapter 5. Jewsbury as a Reviewer and Editor: Forwarding the Cause of Women. 113

Chapter 6. Jewsbury as a Publisher's Reader: Reading for Women. 139

Conclusion. Jewsbury's Legacy: Jewsbury Today 165

Notes 173

Bibliography 177

Index. 187

Acknowledgements

I want to thank the editors of this series, Janine Hatter and Helena Ifill, for recognizing Geraldine Jewsbury's place among the Key Popular Women Writers of the nineteenth century. I also want to thank my friends Carol Durst-Wertheim and AnnaLee Wilson for reading and commenting on chapters of the book as my work progressed. My husband, Roger F. Bloom, has been incredibly understanding during the writing of this book, and I am eternally grateful.

Jeanne Rosenmayer Fahnestock was very generous in discussing Jewsbury with me and providing me with letters and notes originating from Susanne Howe, Jewsbury's biographer. I am also indebted to the librarians and archivists at many libraries and universities, including Rebecca Jewett at Ohio State University; the Alexander Turnbull Library, Wellington, New Zealand; Sarah Hobbs at the Manchester Archives, Manchester Central Library; the National Library of Wales; and Fran Baker at The John Rylands Library. Other scholars, particularly Kathy Chamberlain, Miranda Marraccini, and Beth Rosenberg, have been encouraging and informative.

Material from this book has been presented at two Eighteenth- and Nineteenth-Century British Women Writers Association conferences.

A Note on the Text

I have called Geraldine Jewsbury by her last name throughout the book, but refer to her sister as Maria Jane in order to distinguish between them. Jane Welsh Carlyle is referred to throughout as Welsh Carlyle in order to differentiate her from her husband, Thomas Carlyle. Some spelling errors and typographical mistakes in Jewsbury's writing have been corrected in transcribing her letters, but for the most part I have tried to present them as she wrote them. I have added no emphasis to quotations; all underlining is in the original and appears as italics.

List of Abbreviations

BA, Bentley Archives
CLO, The Carlyle Letters Online
DJO, Dickens Journals Online
GEJ, Geraldine Endsor Jewsbury
JWC, Jane Welsh Carlyle

INTRODUCTION

Rediscovering Geraldine Jewsbury

If women would stand by each other, on the strength of sisterhood ... how much happier would it be in the world for all of them.
—Geraldine Jewsbury to Jane Welsh Carlyle
(5 March 1844, Ireland, 1892: 119)

Geraldine Endsor Jewsbury (1812–80) spent her life working towards a new direction for women. Her beliefs were more aligned with those of feminists of the late-eighteenth and early-nineteenth centuries, such as Mary Wollstonecraft, than the feminists who came to prominence at the end of the nineteenth century when the fight for suffrage became the foremost issue and the term "feminism" came to be used. Like many women of her era, she shied away from political action, but in her life and work she encouraged better education for women, extending employment for women, and legal and societal reform of marriage. She identified the problems facing Great Britain – including spousal abuse, parental rights over children, issues of class, and clerical celibacy – and brought them to light. As Rebecca Solnit states: "diagnosis is the first step towards cure and recovery. To speak of, to find definitions for what afflicted them brought women out of isolation and into power" (2017: 56–57). Jewsbury believed the evolution of the individual would lead inexorably to changes in the structures of society. She did not hold that passing laws to allow equal rights for women was necessary; she assumed change would happen without political engagement. In her time she was a feminist and forged a path for feminists of the future.

Like today, feminism took many forms during the Victorian era, and Jewsbury did not affiliate herself with what was then called the emancipation of women. She claimed not to understand the term "emancipation", writing in a letter: "I have always been quite *content* with getting my own way – and I do not suppose that any of the sex desires more than that and I assure you I never either *write* or talk on that subject – it is quite as much as I can do to take care of myself." (Letter to Mr Sydenham Nodes[?]), 21 July 1851, William Hepworth Dixon Papers, UCLA). Because she took care of herself, having achieved financial independence and a respected place in London literary society, she believed others could do the same. Jewsbury wrote in a review of *Woman: What She Has Been ...*" in 1862: "What is the emancipation of women? – what is it proposed to emancipate them from?" (*Athenaeum*, 2 August 1862: 139). She did not fight to change legal barriers for women, but rather sought to help women throughout her career.

Small, thin, with reddish dark-blonde hair, and beautifully dressed, Jewsbury presented a persona that could always be accepted in society. Ella Hepworth Dixon, a New Woman novelist, wrote of Jewsbury: "Her clothes were of the smartest and made by a modish dressmaker (for Miss Jewsbury was such good company that she stayed in the Seats of the Mighty) and she wore intriguing ear-rings made like miniature parrots, which swayed as she talked" (1930: 13–14). Jewsbury indulged in clothing and enjoyed looking well. Her parrot earrings took away from the seriousness of her accomplishments and revealed a light-hearted aspect of her demeanour. As she did move among "the Seats of the Mighty", in that some of her friends were from the upper classes, and because she worked for male-dominated businesses, she perhaps felt the need to pay careful attention to her toilet. Jewsbury had friends from all walks of life and when she moved to London, she was a successful writer who held a prominent place in literary society and she wanted to retain that position. During the Victorian era women traditionally inhabited the private sphere of the home, leaving men to the public sphere of business. Jewsbury published articles and books and supported herself by working in the world of publishing, an arena traditionally inhabited by men.

During an evening party in 1858, Jewsbury was introduced to an "emancipating" woman. The next day she wrote to her friend Walter Mantell disparaging the woman in a variety of ways. Her first thought is of how unattractive the woman had made herself. She comments that the woman looks "so ungraceful inelegant hard – she *need not* have been ugly – for she had bright piercing intelligent grey eyes – … she wore an extremely *ill fitted* blue satin dress – ill cut – unbecoming a great bow of blue ribbon at the back of her hair looked as if it had been stuck on by way of *protest* against the usages of society" (Dunn, vol. 6, 29 January 1858). The woman undoubtedly dressed herself carefully to show her seriousness as representative of a movement. Jewsbury depicts a stereotype of a feminist that is commonplace even today as a hard, unattractive, unfeminine figure, and she admits that her first thought was: "well I don't suppose any man ever tried to enslave her" (Dunn, vol. 6, 29 January 1858). Jewsbury distances herself from this woman, throwing her under an omnibus as it were, in order to make herself more attractive to the man she wanted to marry.

Her antagonism towards emancipation goes beyond that. Jewsbury separated herself from the emancipated woman in order to claim her own place in male society as a good looking, well-dressed woman who would be acceptable to men. She ends her commentary by writing: "why cannot women make themselves into natural human beings without talking of it till they grow ugly – nobody hinders them except their own abuse & bitter clatter &

gossip about each other – men don't hinder women half so much as women hinder each other – & these emancipating women (all I have seen) look as tho' they had never cared for anybody more than themselves" (Dunn, vol. 6, 29 January 1858). Women hinder the progress of women according to Jewsbury, and perhaps Jewsbury worried that anger directed by the establishment against this emancipated woman, could also be directed against her. Jewsbury faults the woman for not caring about other people, and yet the goal of most emancipated women was to make women the equal of men under the law and in society. Jewsbury thought on a personal, one-on-one, level and attempted to aid both her audience as a writer and her friends with their lives. Jewsbury's anger with the feminist may come from the fact that she did not want to care for herself, that she longed for a man to care for her. Because she realized that she was filled with ambivalence that could not be rationalized, Jewsbury once cautioned Welsh Carlyle: "I was born to drive theories and rules to distraction" ([23 February 1846], Ireland, 1892: 191).

Mary Wollstonecraft emphasized in her *A Vindication of the Rights of Woman*, published in 1792, that women were rational, reasonable beings who ought to be educated to the full extent of their capabilities. Such an education would "enable the individual to attain such habits of virtue as will render it independent" (1792 [1967]: 52). Like Wollstonecraft, Jewsbury emphasized the benefit of education for women and the need for that education to be based on moral principles. In her 1855 novel *Constance Herbert*, a wise older woman proclaims: "it would be an excellent thing if girls had, as far as practicable, the education of boys ... any rational being has reason to regret when the faculties and qualities which God has given him are not called out to the utmost; when anything *less* than the *best* of which he is capable is accepted from him, either in matters of morality or intellect" (1855b: 273–74). Jewsbury believed education must provide morality and consequently, in all her works, she strove to encourage the moral behaviour of her readers.

Jewsbury led a feminist life according to Sara Ahmed's definition: "Living a feminist life does not mean adopting a set of ideals or norms of conduct, although it might mean asking ethical questions about how to live better in an unjust and unequal world (in a not-feminist and antifeminist world); how to create relationships with others that are based on equality; how to find ways to support those who are not supported or are less supported by social systems" (2017: "Introduction"). In her novels and short stories and essays Jewsbury questioned the values of society; in her private life, she sought mentors and became a mentor herself; in her relationships with Jane Welsh Carlyle and Walter Mantell, she created friendships based on equality; and as a reviewer and publisher's reader she attempted to provide women with the means to better themselves and their position within society.

Although Jewsbury lacked the activism of many feminists, she was keenly aware of the difficulties that were "part of the framework in which Victorian feminism developed" as Nancy Cott enumerates them: "The apparent demographic imbalance between men and women, the disinclination of either sex to marry, the problems faced by single women needing to support themselves, the inequities of the marriage laws, the moral consequences of patriarchal marriages and families, the sexual double standard" (1987: 15). Women, during most of the Victorian era, were the property of their fathers until they married when they became the property of their husbands. Early in the era, everything women brought with them into their marriage or produced after it, including their children, belonged to their husbands. Legally, husband and wife were one being, and that being was the husband. Victorian feminists organized in order to change the laws, and Jewsbury made a few public actions in accord with the feminists of the time. In 1856 she signed a petition in support of the Married Women's Property Act along with such prominent women as Jane Welsh Carlyle, Elizabeth

Gaskell, Anna Blackwell, Marian Evans, Harriet Martineau, and Elizabeth Barrett Browning (Rendall, 1985: 143). This measure, to ensure that women had access to their own money and property when married, was not effected until 1870. On another occasion, Jewsbury wrote to Mantell explaining why she distanced herself from women who spoke openly in favour of women's rights: "The women who have taken upon themselves to speak up on behalf of the Women of England (all I have seen of them) women with whom I shd. entirely decline to have any acquaintance women whom I don't either like or admire & by no means my models of female excellence & I am not going to be mixed up with them" (Dunn, vol. 6, 2 February 1858). Again, her words are written to the man she hoped to marry, but she acted in accord with this statement. Jewsbury developed friendships with several women involved in the woman's movement, such as Frances Power Cobb, but Jewsbury worked by herself, as a feminist in her own way, to change the world by changing the women of the future. Jewsbury, like Florence Nightingale and others of her generation, "prided themselves on their independence both from the narrow community of domesticated women and from the newly vocal feminists. They had made their way in the world by hard work, perseverance, and determination, and they were convinced that others could do as well, if only they would try" (Vicinus, 1985: 33). Jewsbury and Nightingale were able to forge their own paths because they were more intelligent, better educated, and more determined than the majority of women.

Although she was uncommon in many ways, Jewsbury did not recognize her unusual qualities and sought to lead the life of an "ordinary" married woman. Her biographer, Susanne Howe, believes she proposed to four different men, Walter Mantell being her last hope for marriage. Jewsbury looked to Walter Mantell to provide a path for her, claiming she had difficulty finding her own way. She wrote to him: "if transmigration of souls were permitted I WD pray to become your Dog that I might call you master – I wd like to *obey* you" (Dunn, vol. 6, 15 January 1858). Yet at other times Jewsbury broke out of that traditional role. She had a passionate nature and when roused, she would speak from her heart. When Mantell was leaving England to go back to New Zealand, Jewsbury wanted him to take her with him and asked him to marry her, an unusual occurrence in the mid-1800s. In her written proposal Jewsbury makes a strong, feminist argument, that positions them as equals: "Is it just that you alone shd have a voice in the fate of both of us? Is not my own happiness & welfare at stake in this matter? – am I a living woman with a reasonable soul & human feelings? Or am I a piece of furniture that you decide on taking or leaving behind?" (Dunn, Vol. 8, 28 August 1859). Rather than a maidenly unformed woman, she describes herself foremost as an accomplished person: "a reasonable soul" with "human feelings". Unfortunately, Jewsbury declared herself to a man who wanted a traditional wife. As women were advancing, they needed men to change as well. Jewsbury recovered from her disappointment and developed a supportive community among other women while leading an independent life of accomplishment.

At the height of Jewsbury's popularity, in 1850, G. H. Lewes listed Jewsbury in an article about female authors: "How many of us can write novels like Currer Bell, Mrs. Gaskell, Geraldine Jewsbury, Mrs. Marsh, Mrs. Crowe and fifty others, with their shrewd and delicate observation of life?" (1850: 189). Although the tone of the article is ironic, Jewsbury appears in the top tier of authors, after Charlotte Brontë, Elizabeth Gaskell, and before two practically-unknown authors and the rest of the horde. After Jewsbury's death the *London Times* ran the following sentence in her obituary: "Many of our readers will regret to learn the intelligence of the death of Miss Geraldine Jewsbury, a lady whose name was well known in the literary world a quarter of a century ago, or perhaps rather more" ("Obituary", 1880: 9). Regarded as a has-been, or a never-was, Jewsbury's fame had decreased since her heyday with her first two novels. She had gone out of the public eye during the latter part of her life because of the anonymity of her jobs as reviewer and publisher's reader. She was to emerge in the public eye again because of the Carlyles.

The "Carlyle controversy" came to a head with the publication of James Anthony Froude's last two volumes of Thomas Carlyle's biography in 1884. These were followed by other publications in which Froude used Jewsbury's conversations with him to make points about Thomas Carlyle's unkindness to his wife, Jane Welsh Carlyle. Froude reported that according to Jewsbury, Carlyle had been violent with his wife, causing bruises on her wrists. In addition, Jewsbury said that Carlyle was the kind of man who never should have married, indicating that he was unable to have sexual intercourse. Several of Carlyle's relatives dismissed Jewsbury's testimony by dwelling on the romantic, flibbertigibbet aspect of Jewsbury. Dr. James Crichton-Browne stated that Jewsbury was a "morbid, unstable, excitable woman" who had inappropriate "erotic" feelings towards Jane Welsh Carlyle (qtd. in Easley, 2011: 165). Carlyle's reputation, as well as Jewsbury's, plummeted.

Jewsbury made many appearances in the memoirs of her contemporaries. S. C. Hall, in 1883, mentions her industry and ability (89–90). Francis Espinasse praises her conversation as "full of wit and point. She was a most agreeable hostess, and never seemed happier than when witnessing the enjoyment of her brother's friends at his frequent symposia" (1893: 136–37). Many friends mention how pleasant it was to spent time with Jewsbury. John Cordy Jeaffreson wrote in 1893:

> In form, presence, air, charm of manner, music of voice, and conversational address, I have never seen Geraldine Jewsbury's equal. Light, lissome, *spirituelle*, her tall, slight figure was singularly graceful… A woman of letters living chiefly if not altogether at the point of her pen, she had need to be mindful of the petty financial economies, but in one direction she was self-indulgent in her personal expenditure.

She enjoyed the favour of a most fashionable millener, whom she honoured as an artist whilst employing her as a dressmaker. (vol. 1, 311)

The impression is similar to that made by Ella Hepworth Dixon in her recollections (1930).

But she was not always remembered positively. In *A Beginner* (1894) Rhoda Broughton, who held a grudge against Jewsbury's opinions of her novels, satirizes Jewsbury as literary critic Miss Grimston, someone who is awkward in society and appears in an "ill-advised gown" and "all-wrong bonnet" (1894: 102; 225). Having written a disaster of a novel herself, Grimston confines herself to "tomahawking" others (1894: 104). The heroine imagines that Grimston instead of mixing with society, is in her room "shrouded with cloud and thunderbolt" (1894: 132). At the end, however, it turns out that Grimston was not the critic who savaged her novel at all. The portrait of Jewsbury that emerged in the late-nineteenth century and early years of the twentieth century is mixed: she is charming in society, she is man-crazy, she is well-dressed, she is not well-dressed, she is a savage critic, and she is ultimately unimportant.

In 1892 Mrs. Alexander Ireland published *Selections from the Letters of Geraldine Endsor Jewsbury to Jane Welsh Carlyle*. As a friend of Geraldine Jewsbury, Ireland felt entitled to change Jewsbury's letters; they are heavily edited and many names have been removed. Ireland also made the letters more regular and less eccentric and consequently removed much of their charm. The originals were destroyed, as were most of the letters from Jane Welsh Carlyle to Jewsbury. Ireland's account of Jewsbury's death suggests the way she wanted to see Jewsbury: "she folded the bright wings so sadly weighted with mortal conflict, closed her once dancing eyes, and slept in peace" (1892: xviii). These letters came to be considered Jewsbury's highest creation and she is most remembered for her friendship with the Carlyles. The Oliphants wrote in 1892: "Miss

Jewsbury wrote two or three novels of the rebellious-sentimental kind, her heroines contending against such contrarieties of fate as that women should have to endure the pains and troubles of maternity. She is chiefly known by her long association and friendship with Thomas Carlyle and his wife" (1892: vol. 2, 191). This has held true into the present day.

Virginia Woolf was fascinated by Jewsbury's letters to Welsh Carlyle and described the woman behind them: "Geraldine Jewsbury herself still survives, independent, courageous, absurd, writing page after page without stopping to correct, and coming out with her views upon love, morality, religion, and the relations of the sexes, whoever may be within hearing, with a cigar between her lips" (1932). Since then, these letters have been examined with the assistance of feminist and lesbian criticism (Cruikshank, 1979; Marcus, 2009; Vicinus, 2004). Many of Jewsbury's letters have not been published. Waldo H. Dunn, a scholar of Carlyle and Froude, transcribed Jewsbury's letters to Walter Mantell held by the Alexander Turnbull Library, Wellington, New Zealand and they were used by Susanne Howe in her 1935 biography of Jewsbury. Joanne Wilkes (1988) and Helene Connor (2001) have also written articles based on Jewsbury's letters to Mantell. Other letters are scattered through many different archives.

In preparation for her biography, Susanne Howe advertised for Jewsbury's letters in the *London Times* and received the following note: "You had much better not write a life of Geraldine Jewsbury. She would be quite forgotten to-day but for her friendship with the Carlyles. Mrs. Ireland's edition of her letters does all that needs to be done to preserve the memory of an entirely unimportant person" (Howe, 1935: vii). Like the Oliphants, this person sees Jewsbury as a footnote to the history of the Carlyles. Howe describes Jewsbury's appeal in her biography:

> She had a taste for experience for its own sake, a rich sense of life and of herself in it. She saw through sham

and pretentiousness with a keenly critical gaze, but she saw too their gorgeous absurdity, and appreciated with an artist's eye their place in the total effect of the human panorama. Unfortunately her literary skill was never equal to her enthusiasm, and so her novels give us only an uneven, undisciplined reproduction of what she saw and felt. But they are authentic and convincing, as she was herself. Her great zest for living made her so. (1935: 202)

Howe interviewed many older people who had seen Geraldine Jewsbury when they were children visiting her room at Walnut Tree House in the company of their parents. What struck them, even in her sickness, was her energy. Her room is described as lovely and piled high with books. She asked about the reading of children and made presents of books. One person remembered her telling fairy tales to them. In all circumstances she paid attention to the young, wanting to educate them towards becoming better people. Howe portrays Jewsbury as a feminist who left no definite work on the subject of women; yet in all of her works, as in her life, Jewsbury was a feminist.

Throughout her adult life, Jewsbury maintained an eminent place in Victorian culture and society and supported herself by literary work. Several considerations of women in Victorian literature mention Jewsbury's novels (Calder, 1976; Showalter, 1977; Gilbert and Gubar, 1979; Foster, 1985). There are also a few studies of individual novels, particularly of her first two novels, *Zoe* (Cary, 1974; Wolff, 1977; Foster, 1989; Rosen, 1996; Werner and Womack, 1997) and *The Half Sisters* (Chattman, 1994; Surridge, 1995; Rosen, 1996; Wilkes, 1994; Lewis, 2003). Scholars have examined her first two novels as influenced by George Sand and Madame de Staël (Thomson, 1977; Surridge, 1995; Lewis, 2003; Stedman, 2011). Jeanne Rosenmayer (later Fahnstock) wrote a dissertation on Jewsbury: "Geraldine Jewsbury: Novelist and Publisher's Reader" (1970). No other work has considered all of Jewsbury's novels in detail. Several scholars have focused on Jewsbury's reviews in the *Athenaeum* (Robinson, 2003; Roberts, 2016) and her reports as a publisher's reader (Gettman, 1960; Griest, 1970; Fahnestock, 1973; Pope, 2013). Other scholars have debated Jewsbury's influence and feminist orientation as a reviewer (Hartley, 1979; Cary, 1974; Fritschner, 1980; Fryckstedt, 1983, 1986; Carney, 1996) and Roberts (2005) looks at all of her writing in this context. Fryckstedt (1985) considers her articles for *Douglas Jerrold's Shilling Magazine*. The threads of Jewsbury's relationships with other women are discussed by Norma Clarke in *Ambitious Heights* (1990) and Julia Marcus in *Across an Untried Sea* (2000). Over time Jewsbury has appeared more favourably in encyclopedia compendiums of British women writers.

This book brings a critical, aesthetic, and historical approach to Jewsbury's works, always keeping her feminism in mind. Because Jewsbury wrote in so many different modes, the chapters are arranged by the genre of Jewsbury's writing, while showing how her thoughts carry over from one part of her life into another. Before she began publishing, two writers played a major role in forming Jewsbury. Chapter 1, "Early Influences: Becoming Geraldine Jewsbury", looks at the impact that her sister, Maria Jane Jewsbury, and her reading of Thomas Carlyle, had on her. Born in Meacham, England and raised in Manchester, Jewsbury was just six years old when her mother died in 1818. Jewsbury was brought up by her sister, Maria Jane Jewsbury (born 1800). Maria Jane modeled for her sister how to manage domestic duties while writing and how to continue writing productively whatever your mental or physical situation. Yet because of the difference in their ages, they were never equals. The marriage and death of Maria Jane in 1833 left Jewsbury as the housekeeper for their father and the overseer of their younger brothers. During her years as caretaker for the Jewsbury family, Maria Jane contacted William Wordsworth and developed a deep friendship with his daughter, Dora, a pattern that Jewsbury repeated by writing to Thomas

Carlyle during her tenure as caretaker and then becoming friends with his wife, Jane Welsh Carlyle. The death of their father in 1840 allowed Jewsbury to reside with her beloved brother Frank in an area outside of Manchester where they established literary relationships with people such Ralph Waldo Emerson, George Henry Lewes, and the actress Charlotte Cushman. While living in Manchester, Jewsbury began to publish articles in journals and newspapers.

Chapter 2, "The Carlyles and *Zoe*: Discovering the World", explores Jewsbury's early publications and her first novel, *Zoe: The History of Two Lives* (1845). An historical novel set in the eighteenth century, *Zoe* examines both skepticism over the orthodox tenets of religion and the future of women who were well-educated but without careers. Jewsbury achieved fame and notoriety with *Zoe*, which began as a means of keeping together a long-distance friendship between Elizabeth Paulet, Jane Welsh Carlyle, and herself. Eventually Paulet and Welsh Carlyle dropped out of the writing, but Welsh Carlyle assisted with creating the final draft of the manuscript and providing Jewsbury with an introduction to the publisher. Welsh Carlyle laboured to give *Zoe* and Jewsbury decency, but the novel was still considered scandalous in its time.

Following the publication of *Zoe*, Jewsbury wrote five novels for adults and two for children. Chapter 3, "Fiction and Short Pieces: Educating Readers", examines these works. *The Half Sisters* (1848) features two half-sisters, one of whom marries and finds herself tempted by an affair because she believes herself to be neglected by her husband, while the other becomes a famous actress who ultimately marries an enlightened man. *Marian Withers* (1851), set in Manchester, makes use of the manufacturing concerns Jewsbury was familiar with from childhood. *Constance Herbert* (1855b) involves the problems of inherited insanity and the need to do one's duty rather than that which might bring personal happiness. *The Sorrows of Gentility* (1856) reveals the trappings of false gentility and the need for education based on one's sphere of life. *Right or Wrong* (1859b) questions the celibacy of the clergy. Two novels for children, *The History of an Adopted Child* (1852) and *Angelo, or The Pine Forest in the Alps* (1855a), depict many of the ideas about the importance of mentors and education found in her novels for adults. This chapter also considers a few of Jewsbury's short stories and articles which take up the themes she introduced in her longer fiction but look more closely at problems of class rather than gender. In these works Jewsbury sought to encourage her readers to lead rational, moral lives.

Through all of her life, Jewsbury wrote letters to friends and acquaintances. Chapter 4, "Letters: Jane Welsh Carlyle, Walter Mantell, and Other Friendships", looks at Jewsbury's bonds with her acquaintances. Jewsbury's feminism, her thoughts on women and their situation in the world, is most strongly expressed in her letters to Welsh Carlyle (published by Mrs. Alexander Ireland and covering the years 1841–52), where Jewsbury could write openly and passionately. Jewsbury wrote over 500 letters between 1836 and 1880, the year of her death, to Walter Mantell (Alexander Turnbull Library, Wellington, New Zealand). Although Mantell moved to New Zealand and married, they remained good friends. The third set of her letters discussed are written to a young woman in Wales, Betha Johnes, whom she befriended and influenced (National Library of Wales).

Jewsbury's letters and correspondence with friends and professional contacts reveal the life and career of a single and busy mid-Victorian woman. Her letters are lively, readable, and emotionally open. In them she seeks to explain herself, to find intimacy, and most of all to make a community for herself where she can be honest, appreciated, and help others. As a surplus or redundant, single woman, Jewsbury turned to friends for the ideas and conversation she might have found with members of a family. In an era in which women were silenced, marginalized, and dedicated to the home, many found strength in numbers. Feminists have often been drawn to communities as a way of gaining support against restrictive environments. During the Victorian era, women banded together in order to provide a space for themselves for different activities, often for the purpose of changing society. For example, The Langham Place Circle formed in the 1850s in London in order to advocate for rights for women and also to provide a place where members could meet, study, and work. Many groups were more specialized or more informal. Jewsbury's sister, Maria Jane Jewsbury, had formed a community with Mrs. Hemans to encourage each other to write and Jewsbury had witnessed their cooperation as a young girl. This was the same kind of support and friendship that Jewsbury attempted to achieve with Elizabeth Paulet and Jane Welsh Carlyle in order to write a novel, but because they lived far apart, they planned to pass the manuscript to each other by mail as they added to it. Although that attempt failed, Jewsbury continued to form close friendships.

As a reviewer, Jewsbury made use of her intricate knowledge of novels. Chapter 5, "Jewsbury as a Reviewer and Editor: Forwarding the Cause of Women", explores some of her approximately 2310 reviews published in the *Athenaeum* between 1849 and 1880. Although some personal idiosyncrasy may be discerned (in her letters she states she preferred the fiction of G. H. Lewes to Charlotte Brontë's *Jane Eyre*), her reviews were influential. Jewsbury's involvement in the publication of the memoirs of Lady Morgan (1862) and Caroline Herschel (1875) reveals the importance that she placed on the lives of women.

Chapter 6, "Jewsbury as a Publisher's Reader: Reading for Women", follows her impact on a major Victorian publishing house, Bentley and Son, for whom she read manuscripts and gave recommendations on their publications from 1849 until a few weeks before she died. She read over 800 manuscripts, predominantly commenting on novels written by women and recommending them for a female readership that included Mudie's Circulating Library. She knew literature influenced the way that women thought and so believed fervently in controlling what young women read, preferring books that show women who lived like themselves and whose decisions would be of benefit to readers in their own lives. Jewsbury commented on several works that became best sellers, including *East Lynne* by Ellen Wood (1861), *Lady Audley's Secret* by Mary Elizabeth Braddon (1862), *Not Wisely but Too Well* by Rhoda Broughton (1867), and *Under Two Flags* by Ouida (1867). Although she desired to recommend great literature, she encountered too many manuscripts that were poorly written, or written without what Jewsbury saw as a clear moral purpose. As a publisher's reader, Jewsbury took a new course in finding a platform for her voice and a means of supporting herself within a system that she bent but did not break.

The Conclusion, "Jewsbury's Legacy: Jewsbury Today", looks at why Jewsbury is so little known today, the importance of Jewsbury's work for us, the place for Jewsbury in the classroom and on the bookcase, and the need for more discussion of Jewsbury. As a journalist, novelist, essayist, short story writer, letter writer, editor, reviewer, publisher's reader, and friend, Jewsbury examined the way women should live their lives and the difficulties and limited opportunities available to them. She wrote a large amount, much of it anonymously, and portions of her work remain unknown. Even though she did not exhibit her beliefs and attitudes like the emancipated woman with the blue bow, Jewsbury was a feminist in her own time.

Jewsbury wrote novels, articles, short stories, letters, reviews, and reader's reports, and feminist themes run through them all. Feminists of the 1960s and 1970s often stated that "The personal is political" (Ahmed, 2017: "Introduction") and thus in her private life as in her writing, Jewsbury promoted the mentoring of women by women and friendship among women. The advancement of women in the nineteenth century, as in the twentieth and twenty-first centuries, meant different things to different people. Chimamanda Ngozi Adichie in her TED talk "We should all be feminists" defined a feminist as someone who says: "Yes, there's a problem with gender as it is today, and we must fix it. We must do better" (2012). Geraldine Jewsbury definitely saw and described the problems of gender in her society and worked to improve the lives of women.

Through the work of many people during the nineteenth century, women slowly gained more rights and power. Laws were changed, education was improved, and women joined the work force in ways they had not done before. One of the influences behind this advancement was individual women who in their own ways prepared the way for other women. Geraldine Endsor Jewsbury was such a woman. This book examines her life and work in order to show the ways she provided a new direction for women.

CHAPTER 1

Early Influences: Becoming Geraldine Jewsbury

> There is something hard, not natural, in all women who have had no mother!
> —Geraldine Jewsbury to Jane Welsh Carlyle
> ([23 February 1846], Ireland, 1892: 189)

Geraldine Endsor Jewsbury was well aware of the difficulties of women who had no mothers. She believed that women without mothers were "not treated kindly" and "driven within" themselves ([23 February 1846], Ireland, 1892: 189). In many ways Jewsbury's life was a struggle to find a mentor from whom she could receive kindness, and a community in which she felt supported. She treated others sympathetically, especially women and servants, as she was always aware of their difficulties. She was the fourth child of Thomas and Maria Smith Jewsbury, born in Measham, Derbyshire (now Leicestershire) on 22 August 1812. The family moved to Manchester in 1816 where their father, formerly an independent cotton mill owner, became a cotton merchant and insurance agent. The youngest child, Francis (known as Frank), was born in 1819 and their mother died a month later. Jewsbury wrote to her friend Walter Mantell when she was forty-five: "I envy everybody who has a mother – Mine died when I was 6 years old & I feel to miss her more every year I live, one wd have been so different" (Dunn, vol. 2, 22 March 1857). Rather than sympathy and love, Jewsbury felt her childhood had been filled with unkindness and made her "hard".

Upon the death of their mother, Jewsbury's older sister, Maria Jane, then nineteen years old, was called upon to keep house for their father and to be a substitute mother for the children. Maria Jane had received a limited education but had the desire to write from the time she was young. Expected to perform the chores of a wife and mother without any compensating elevation of status in a home not of her own making, Maria Jane ordered dinners, supervised the servants, and attended to the children. She described the situation to a friend soon after she took over the household, always thinking of her desire for writing along with her duties: "Three dear children are catechizing me at the rate of ten questions in every five minutes. I am within hearing of one servant stoning a kitchen floor; and of another practising a hymn; and of a very turbulent child and unsympathetic nurse next door. I think I could make a decent paper descriptive of the miseries of combining literary tastes with domestic duties" (Gillette, 1932: xvii-xviii). In addition to her sister and the infant Frank, Maria Jane was responsible for Thomas then seventeen, Henry then sixteen, and Arthur then three. Despite the distractions of the household, Maria Jane persisted in literary pursuits and in 1821 contributed to the *Manchester Gazette* and the *Manchester Courier*. Eventually she published many poems, as well as prose pieces, in local as well as London periodicals, and gift annuals, all written while tending to the Jewsbury family. She was also employed as a book reviewer for the *Athenaeum*, as Jewsbury was to be later. Maria Jane trained Jewsbury in housekeeping and cooking skills that enabled her to entertain with ease as an adult, showed her how to manage a household with little money, and patterned a process of becoming a productive writer while finding support from other women.

Little information is available about the particulars of Jewsbury's childhood and youth. Certainly the death of her mother had a major impact on her life. She rarely mentions her father in her letters and she does not describe her sister with affection. Never indulged, Jewsbury was brought up to put her own desires aside, to be "sensible" and to expect little from life. On being taken to the opera, she was told "in all likelihood you will *never* go again". Recollecting this event later in life, she wrote to Walter Mantell that what was so painful was "not the passing *away* of the pleasure but the *wooden horizon* that was set up" (Dunn, vol. 2, 4 August 1857). At another time she wrote to Mantell: "You don't know how cruel people were to me when I was living at home as a young girl who *might* for *every* reason to have shown me kindness & help". Since Maria Jane was besieged by so many other children and chores, Jewsbury may have been often left to the care of servants. In the same letter to Mantell, Jewsbury describes making a petticoat for a servant "who used to *snub* me when I was ten years old and then lived with me as *my* mistress for seven long years scolding me & tyrannizing over me dreadfully except when I chanced to be ill" (Dunn, vol. 6, 8 January 1857). Although made miserable when she was a child by the servant, as an adult Jewsbury forgave her tormenter and helped her. A sensitive and emotional child, Jewsbury must have felt short-changed in her need for attention and affection. Yet this neglect forced her to be independent and "hard". As an adult, Jewsbury wrote to a friend: "I used to cry to be carried, indeed I have had a great taste for it all my life, but I have been made to find my own feet" (Howe, 1935: 19). During the Victorian era, women were taught to be soft and malleable. Both Jewsbury and Maria Jane were hard in that they were determined and independent, and both disliked this tendency in themselves.

While Jewsbury turned in to herself, her sister laboured to become known in the world. In 1825 Maria Jane published a book of poems and essays, *Phantasmagoria*, and dedicated them to William Wordsworth. She sent a copy to the famous poet asking for his advice. He responded, inviting her to visit him and his family, which she did. This event transformed her life. She became a welcomed member of the Wordsworth household and developed a close friendship with Dora Wordsworth, the poet's daughter. She was not treated as an "equal" by Wordsworth; the women in his household buttressed the poet and Maria Jane comments on Wordsworth's ideas of the "pains & penalties of female authorship" in a letter addressed to Dora (Wordsworth Trust, 20 January 1829). In a similar vein to Wordsworth, the Poet Laureate, Robert Southey, pointed out the inadvisability of female authorship to Charlotte Brontë in a letter from 1837:

> The day dreams in which you habitually indulge are likely to induce a distempered state of mind; and, in proportion as all the ordinary uses of the world seem to you flat and unprofitable, you will be unfitted for them without becoming fitted for anything else. Literature cannot be the business of a woman's life, and it ought not to be. The more she is engaged in her proper duties, the less leisure will she have for it, even as an accomplishment and a recreation. (Barker, 1994: 262)

People in nineteenth-century England generally believed that women were ordained by God, since Eve was created from Adam's rib, to be the helpmates of men. Societal beliefs of women as passive and unintellectual melded into the ideal that became known as the "Angel in the House" after Coventry Patmore's 1854 poem, which celebrated woman's traditional spiritual role. A young woman was to take care of her husband or her family, to guide the religious beliefs and education of her family, and to present a moral example to all in her activities and statements; in return she would be cared for financially and physically by her father until she married and then by her husband. Writing, with its involvement with publishers and audiences, was a masculine activity that was believed to harden the female. Both Maria Jane and Jewsbury were to suffer from the difficulties of being blue stockings and female writers; although they rebelled against such stereotypical beliefs, they also fell victim to them.

Described by contemporaries in almost masculine terms, Maria Jane had a decisive temperament and firm ideas. She wrote and sought publication, but she at times doubted herself and desired to submit to God's plan for her. Comparing herself with Wordsworth, she worried that she might not be a good enough writer to make a successful career possible. Renown, the support of other creative women, and financial independence were not enough. Although Maria Jane and Jewsbury were to sound and behave like feminists at times, they were too much indoctrinated by their societies to actively support female emancipation. Jewsbury had an advantage over her sister in that she began publishing almost twenty years later than Maria Jane, when opinions were starting to change. Both women lived independently and productively while claiming to be opposed to the ideas of women who openly supported female emancipation and equality.

Writing under the difficulties of supervising a home and children while entertaining high ambition, Maria Jane and Jewsbury were both to suffer from exhaustion and mental crises. Maria Jane wrote to Dora Wordsworth in 1825 sending her a poem, "A Farewell to the Muse", and stating that she was "tired of writing *pretty verses*". Aware of her lack of formal education, Maria Jane intended to continue her own education with independent reading. She complains that "Hitherto my life has been a series of sacrifices" (8 October 1825, Wordsworth Trust). In November of 1826 Maria Jane became ill and left Manchester to be nursed back to health by friends. Being ill allowed Maria Jane a chance to rest and to ease her burden of care for others. Since Jewsbury's education could no longer be supervised by Maria Jane, Jewsbury was placed in the Miss Darby's boarding school in Tamworth, Staffordshire.

While at school Jewsbury wrote one letter a week to different members of her family but these letters have not survived. However, peripheral information about Jewsbury can be gathered from Maria Jane's letters to her. Maria Jane wanted Jewsbury to be prepared to support herself. As a middle-class Victorian woman, there were only three choices available for Jewsbury's adult life: she could marry and be supported by a husband, she could become a teacher or governess or seamstress, or she could continue to be supported by her father or brothers. Maria Jane was adamant that Jewsbury should work hard and excel at her studies in order to secure employment as a governess because Jewsbury did not want to be a teacher. In her letters to her sister, Maria Jane emphasizes the importance of religion, the need for Jewsbury to submit to the will of God and to renunciate any earthly desires she might indulge. Maria Jane must have thought that by limiting Jewsbury's horizon, she was being realistic about her future.

In every letter to Jewsbury, Maria Jane shows concern for her education, for a correct frame of mind, but never unconditional love. Although Maria Jane praises Jewsbury for making progress, she advises her sister that the more she improves, the more she will love her. Worried that Jewsbury is too pleased with herself for doing well at school, Maria Jane criticizes her in a moralistic manner: "to pass your companions, to be acknowledged clever, to win prizes, no matter for what so it do but include competition, and procure triumph; this is the little Babylon you are now building ..." (qtd. Jump, 1999a: 70). Even though Jewsbury won prizes at school, Maria Jane's concern was with her attitude – she should do well so that she can get employment not so as to show herself superior to others.

While Maria Jane compliments Jewsbury's affection and good nature, she criticizes Jewsbury's writing "& *occasional* spelling". Harriet Devine Jump has pointed out the frequency with which Maria Jane commented on Jewsbury's poor penmanship. In one of Maria Jane's letters to Jewsbury she encloses an older girl's letter: "to read, if it were only that you might admire the *handwriting* &

resolve to mend your own! ... I am uneasy to receive such pothooks and hangers as your letters comprise" (qtd. Jump, 1999a: 66); and "Do not in your letters underline so many words – scarcely any" (qtd. Jump, 1999a: 66). Jewsbury's handwriting, including her spelling and means of expression, would be the first obstacle to her finding employment as a governess. Her punctuation and use of emphasis never improved, but Jewsbury's writing would later become the means of her creativity and the expression of her individual self.

In her criticisms of Jewsbury, Maria Jane most frequently points out her need for self-control. She fears that Jewsbury lacks the requisite character for teaching: "patience & temper!" Attempting to correct Jewsbury's attitude, she wishes above all that Jewsbury "speak of [her] faults with less flippancy" (September 1827, John Rylands Library). Maria Jane complains that Jewsbury is "not good at conveying facts" and notices that Jewsbury is in a "feverish disquieted state" and has an "ardent ambitious temper" that needs to be conquered (September 1827, John Rylands Library). Maria Jane praises a young lady who has gone out as a governess at seventeen and turns the lesson pointedly to Jewsbury while describing Miss Dale who has "made the most of her advantages":

> Independent of being personally provided for, she will be enabled to assist her family. I tell you all this my dear child, that you maybe encouraged to exert yourself – since you see here the pleasing consequences of exertion & painstaking. I do not mean to say that every girl, educated – provided for herself, will meet with *equal* success – by no means – but as an axiom, industry will almost invariably obtain a portion. (28 March 1827, John Rylands Library)

Writing about Jewsbury to Dora Wordsworth, Maria Jane expresses her "ambition" for her sister:

> [She] has now Miss D.[Darby] tells me capacity of gaining a salary, & is fitted for one or two *little girls* – This is my ambition for her – in a genteel, kind, *good*, family – she draws now in a masterly style – dances – is a tolerable Italian & an excellent French scholar … let me know if in your travels you hear of any family *of the kind I mean* … for many places she is too pretty – & young. I must have a sober minded family – & if they would be kind to her – & if under their roof and influence & example she would be silently maturing & deriving *moral* benefit, salary should *not* be the great object. (Wordsworth Trust, 3 February 1831)

Maria Jane seeks a family who will take care of Jewsbury and improve her morals. She might have praised Jewsbury's spirit, personality, intelligence, and imagination, her unusual qualities, but Maria Jane believed her duty was to prepare Jewsbury to support herself and to make sure her soul was ready for heaven. That Maria Jane's ambition for her sister was restricted to making a small amount of money in an insecure job reveals the limited possibilities available for women in the nineteenth century. Jewsbury herself was to address this issue and the problems of education for women in her writing career. Recognizing that her own aspirations needed to be tamped down, but directing her words to her sister, Maria Jane wrote birthday wishes to Jewsbury in 1827 on her fifteenth birthday: "The wreath of Fame is often a fiery crown, burning the brows that wear it – I do my dear love wish you all *good* things on your birthday – and amongst them moderated expectations of life" (Clarke, 1990: 70). Jewsbury, home from school when she was sixteen, was described by her sister to Felicia Hemans as: "a sweet girl, with a woeful [?] turn for composition, but practical & very modest" (10 July 1827, John Rylands Library).[1] She is able to "make breakfast for poor father, and read to him at night, and so make amends for my lack of service" (Clarke, 1990: 72) and she is "sweet & docile" (Wordsworth Trust, 23 July 1829). Jewsbury receives credit for being useful, feminine, and passive.

In 1828, while recovering from ill health, Maria Jane published her *Letters to the Young*, a kind of self-help book in a popular format preparing the young, particularly women, for becoming responsible and moral adults by abjuring fame and submitting to religion. The book was inspired in part by her letters to Jewsbury. Angela Leighton and Margaret Reynolds see a subversive message in Maria Jane's production of *Letters to the Young* "in the suggestion that sickness is one route which may allow control of one's intellectual environment because it means opting out of the real world of domesticity and the marriage market" (1995: 27). Maria Jane had come out of her sickness with this manuscript in hand. Many Victorian women, such as Florence Nightingale and Elizabeth Barrett Browning, wrote from their sickrooms with the advantage of not having to take part in the rounds of visiting, entertaining, and other duties imposed on young women. Although the start of the illness may well have been physical or emotional, Victorian women had real incentive to delay recovery as more of their own work could be done while they were convalescing and exempt from household tasks.

The ideas of "moderated expectations of life" and submission to the will of God that Maria Jane propounded to Jewsbury are themes running through Maria Jane's book. As Jump highlights, the text of the letters indicates that they were written to different, unnamed, recipients and "the whole object of the book … is designed to apply to a variety of different cases and circumstances rather than, as has been previously suggested, haranguing one unfortunate individual [namely Jewsbury] through the whole of its 240 pages" (1999a: 65–66). In one of the *Letters to the Young*, Maria Jane addresses a particular young woman on her flaws: "characters of softer, meeker mould, make more progress and do more good, with far less grace, than will suffice for a being whose 'events are emotions;' whose principles are impulses; whose feelings are passions; whose changes are contradictions; to whose whole moral existence enthusiasm is a never setting sun" (1835: 181). Howe perceives this as a criticism of Jewsbury, who was always enthusiastic and emotional. From the point of view of Maria Jane, if Jewsbury were softer and meeker, she would be more pliable, easier to govern, and more fit for heaven.

Maria Jane had the ability to turn acquaintances into friends, and Jewsbury shared this trait. Over the course of Jewsbury's education, both Maria Jane and Jewsbury developed a closeness with Jewsbury's teachers, the Miss Darbys. In 1830 Jewsbury stayed at the Misses Darby's home in London and studied Italian and drawing in order to finish her training for becoming a governess. In the evenings Maria Jane introduced her to literary friends. These were happy times for the sisters when they were involved with something that mattered to them both: literature. Jewsbury would correspond with the Miss Darbys as long as they lived, and later traveled to assist one of them when she needed help.

The sisters did enjoy leisure time together. Late in her life Jewsbury recounted to Mantell that she had met a middle aged man and been reminded of a vacation taken with her sister and brothers when she was sixteen:

> a short – grave, care-worn furrowed middle aged man came up & making a bow said 'Miss Jewsbury?' – yes – & you are – 'Mr. Hemans – George?' 'Yes' – he sat down beside me & we *looked at each other*! – years ago more years than I care to count when I was a very young girl my sister went into Wales to spend the summer – I was sent for to spend my holidays in the cottage with her – & my two brothers Arthur & Frank came too – Mrs. Hemans lived at Rhyllon about a mile from us she lived with her brother & sister & her *five boys* ... – we had a very pleasant time & we used to go to & fro from the cottage to Rhyllon Mrs H's house every day. (Dunn, vol. 6, [18 April 1858])

Maria Jane had formed a close friendship with Mrs. Hemans who was also a poet. During their vacation the women spent time writing. Jewsbury was able to observe the importance of friendship and community to her sister's work, a condition that Jewsbury replicated later in her life.

Maria Jane published many poems in newspapers and annuals[2] as well as a series of "Provincial Letters" and reviews in the *Athenaeum*. She wrote four books: *Phantasmagoria or Sketches of Life in Literature* (1825); *Letters to the Young* (1828); *Lays of Leisure Hours* (1829); and the *Three Histories* (1830). The heroine of Maria Jane's most interesting work, *Three Histories*, is a celebrated writer. However, in choosing to become a writer, she loses the man she loves to a less accomplished woman. Like Maria Jane, Jewsbury never created a heroine who had both a career and a happy marriage at the same time. In a study of women during the early Victorian era, Clarke identifies an "incompatibility of literary ambition and wifely duty" (1990: 14). Frequently, women who marry do not continue to have literary ambitions or do not write. Other popular women writers, like Mrs. Hemans and Margaret Oliphant, were forced to write in order to support themselves and their children following the death or desertion of their husbands. However, Maria Jane and Jewsbury both desired to marry.

In August of 1832, when she was over thirty, Maria Jane married the Reverend William Kew Fletcher, after having refused him and telling Dora Wordsworth that she was not in love with him. A friend wrote an account of the wedding: "Geraldine was, of course, the Bride's maid, and looked very pretty even through her tears. She has behaved delightfully throughout the whole affair, with entire forgetfulness of self, and thinking only how she could relieve and serve her sister" (Gillette, 1932: lix). Mrs. Wordsworth wrote to Mr. Jewsbury after Maria Jane's marriage, attempting to console him for the loss of his older daughter: "we must not forget what a treasure you have left in your other daughter" (Howe, 1935: 19). Following their marriage Maria Jane's husband was assigned to a ministry in India and they left England in September and landed in Bombay in March 1833. Maria Jane died of cholera in India on 4 October 1833. Her friends believed that Maria Jane never achieved her potential as a writer. She had taken many of her literary papers, both published without her name and unpublished, with her to India. Her widowed husband never communicated with the Jewsbury family and never returned Maria Jane's papers although Jewsbury wanted to bring out a collection of her writings. Many years later, Mr. Fletcher's second wife returned the papers to Jewsbury.

Maria Jane had forged a friendship with Mrs. Hemans, the most well-known female poet of her era, and developed a community of women writers both inside and outside Manchester that provided support for each other. Geraldine Jewsbury was to accomplish something similar with the friendship of Jane Welsh Carlyle. Clarke states:

> In many ways, her [Jewsbury's] formative years with the first Jane (as Maria Jane was generally known) structured her friendship with the second. The two Janes were in any case remarkably alike in significant ways. Exact contemporaries, both were intellectual women of outgoing not retiring dispositions. Both were satirical and sharp; both had characteristics others labelled 'masculine'. They shared a love of truth, a dislike of hypocrisy, and a deflating sense of humour. In both cases, their energy and assurance of self led to them being regarded as 'unfeminine' ... If Jane Carlyle was a women of genius silenced by marriage to a towering man of genius, Jane Jewsbury, who never stopped writing, was just as effectively silenced by marriage to the rather humdrum Revd William K. Fletcher. (1990: 10–11)

What struck people about Maria Jane was her conversation and the liveliness of her mind, much as Welsh Carlyle was to impress people. Both were remembered more for what they could have achieved than for what they did produce.

With the departure of Maria Jane, Jewsbury became the female head of her father's household as her sister had been before her. She was just twenty, a few months older than Maria Jane had been when their mother died and she had taken over the household. Jewsbury wrote to Thomas Carlyle many years later: "When my sister left, though I was turned twenty I had made no acquaintance of my own standing and was so childish both in manner and appearance that I could expect nothing from her friends beyond mere good-natured notice" (Howe, 1935: 19). At this time Jewsbury struggled with a mental crisis that had its onset several years before. Since she was sixteen Jewsbury had set herself on a course of reading metaphysics with the desire to write about "matter and spirit". Little is known about this crisis other than Jewsbury's description to her friend Jane Welsh Carlyle later in her life:

> ... when I got into my desperate condition, from which I was barely emerging when you first saw me, I endeavoured to drown my pain, not by inditing a 'diary of an ennuyée,' but by writing an essay on materialism, ... before I finally abandoned myself to despair and hysterics; from all which it may be seen, that when people have cause for unhappiness, it is no good for them to try and cheat themselves. It must come on and be regularly worn out – 'exploited,' as you call it So you see there is nothing marvelous in my philosophy! I learnt the best part of it when I was very miserable, more miserable than one human being can be twice in one lifetime.
> ([12 February 1844], Ireland, 1892: 103–04)

Like Maria Jane, Jewsbury struggled with religious questions, but the answer she eventually arrived at was far different from the traditional approach to religion Maria Jane found. In her struggles, Jewsbury was helped by Thomas Carlyle whose writings describe his disbelief followed by feelings of loss and eventual recovery. She would reach out to him for advice. No woman had written about religious struggles – Jewsbury would be the first one in her novel *Zoe*. Jewsbury had broad interests and approached them directly. Her manner, like Maria Jane's, was neither passive nor traditionally feminine. Jewsbury may have needed to harden herself as she turned inward and looked for help during this difficult time.[3]

With her brothers grown, Jewsbury had to worry about her future as a young woman who either had to marry, find a means to support herself, or continue to be cared for by her father or brothers. In order to take action, Jewsbury needed to escape the passivity induced by her depression and loss of traditional religious faith. She inundated herself with difficult readings and the result was an essay on materialism, the start of her literary career. What became of this essay is unclear; it may have been transformed into her review essay, "Religious Faith and Modern Scepticism", published years later in 1850. In her reading Jewsbury had been impressed by the essay "Characteristics" (1831) and the novel *Sartor Resartus* (1833–34) by Thomas Carlyle. Discovering similarities in her thought to his, she wrote to Carlyle for help in getting past the isolation and pain of her loss of belief. Jewsbury repeated the pattern taken by her sister of being helped forward by a well-established writer and making an emotional attachment with a woman of his family; in Jewsbury's case with Carlyle's wife, Jane Welsh Carlyle. This provided both sisters with a feminine and acceptable role approved by their mentors.

Seeking relief from her unquietness of mind, Jewsbury was drawn to Carlyle because, as she wrote in an essay published in 1850: "Thomas Carlyle, in his 'Sartor Resartus', was the first who recognised in print the fact that a man may be at once religious of heart and skeptical of doctrine. He was the first man in England who dared to declare that a sincere *doubt* was as much entitled to respect as a sincere *belief*. He treated with *respect* certain conditions of heart which had hitherto been met with grave reprobation" ("Religious Faith and Modern Scepticism", 1850a: 205). In *Sartor Resartus*, Carlyle's fictional hero, Diogenes Teufelsdröckh, travels from The Everlasting No through the Centre of Indifference to The Everlasting Yea as he rejects traditional religion, becomes depressed, and eventually comes to believe in doing without happiness and accepts renunciation.

Jewsbury first wrote to Thomas Carlyle on 6 April 1840 wondering how he found faith of a non-traditional kind to substitute for traditional religion:

> – it cannot be that you, who describe with such true knowledge, the mental state of those who have left the beaten track of Creeds and Catechisms, should not have also seen some conclusion of the whole matter; through all the struggles that you recognize, there seems to be some strong unwavering Faith in some Spiritual Presence wh. lies enshrined not in man alone, but pervading all Nature, a Spiritual Power, apart from a higher than mere Life, the unintelligent vitality wh. works within all things, from inherent energy and necessity: but you no-where tell us how you have attained this Faith; – plunge into what speculations you will, so long as you retain this, you have in your hand a clue wh. if followed, will in due time lead you thro' the Labarynth. (Rosenmayer, 1970: 49)[4]

She goes on to describe the difficulty with which she shook off religion and then the resulting deliverance followed by the desolation of having no belief. Jewsbury was stuck in the Centre of Indifference and sought help in moving forward.

Carlyle was obviously taken with the sincerity of her words and responded in a manner both impersonal and personal: "'G.E.J.,' whom I will take to be a Lady, of cultivated intellect, of clear conscientious character, between twenty and thirty, describes, with energy sincerity and evident truth to nature, a spiritual history which is very painful, which to those that understand it cannot be other than interesting" (CLO, 12 April 1840). He foresees that she will, as he has, achieve victory. But, he continues, there is really nothing he can say that will make it easier for her. He recommends that she learn German and read Goethe and that she read his description of a similar journey in *Sartor Resartus* (which she had already read), that she do the duty that lies nearest at hand, and she undertake not to seek happiness, that she submit to God and follow the truth. Jewsbury asks which German books he would recommend and whether it were possible to read them in translation as that would be quicker than learning German (CLO, 18 April 1840). Directing Jewsbury's reading was a familiar role for Carlyle as a former teacher and tutor who supervised the reading of Jane Welsh before she became his wife.

In other letters to Carlyle, Jewsbury complains of her isolation. She was not surrounded by like-minded people; she was residing with her father, a man dedicated to business. She admits that she finds it difficult to talk to anyone in her circle about her skepticism and mentions Mrs. Paulet (who would play an important role in the creation of her first novel) as her only intimate friend. Carlyle reassures her: "Fear nothing, dear young friend, except your own impatience of heart: one's own poor egoism, hungry love of Happiness &c, is the only thing one has to fear. I rejoice to believe that you are not one of those for whom such noble disease is appointed to end not in health, victory, enlargement, but in chronic sickness, in mere hollow truce, or peace by surrender" (CLO, 26 April 1840). Jewsbury seeks a means of answering her own doubts while Carlyle responds that she can read what others have written on these subjects, including his own translations, but that she must travel her own path as there is no set answer. In some ways they are writing past each other. Carlyle's approach is general and intellectual while Jewsbury yearns for an emotional connection and exact answers.

In her letters Jewsbury mentions her own belief that passions that are strong and real are sacred (Rosenmayer, 1970: 52). In his response Carlyle expresses his sympathy for her suffering, assuring her of the "image of an honest, clear, energetic, humbly and nobly resolute soul" and that "all growth is sickly, painful". He believes she must suffer and work out a personal and incomplete answer for herself (CLO, 15 June 1840), but affirms that she will eventually triumph. When Jewsbury writes about passions, she is probably referring to both strong emotions and sexual desire, but she broaches an area Carlyle is not comfortable with and he once again directs her reading without responding to her mention of passion.

Jewsbury asks him: "Why must we thus labour day after day to perfect ourselves? to what purpose are we struggling?" (Rosenmayer, 1970: 54). When he states that the question cannot be answered, she presses him for a more explicit understanding as to how and why changes occur: "Do you think the highest gifts can be possessed unconsciously for any length of time? Till a time of need arises a man be unaware of his capacity to meet emergencies ..." (Rosenmayer, 1970: 55). Thomas Carlyle responds with a letter beginning: "Your letters awaken in me many thoughts; many feelings, among which affectionate interest in you, sympathy and hope for you, occupy a prime place". Carlyle has compassion for Jewsbury but expresses himself in generalities, reflecting on the words: "unconsciousness, Silence" that are so difficult to discuss (CLO, 5 September 1840). He suggests she come to visit him and his wife in London.

Shortly after this, in 1840, Jewsbury's father died and Jewsbury went to live with her brother Frank in the rural area of Greenheys outside of Manchester.[5] Like their father, the younger Jewsbury men were involved in business ventures, except for Arthur, who having quarreled with his family, had gone to sea and was seldom heard from again. But Frank had an interest in literature and developed a literary circle of friends. Jewsbury was immediately popular within her brother's circle as Mrs. Everett Green recollected, Jewsbury "possessed the gift of fascinating young and old, learned and unlearned, servants included ... her manner was so piquant and original and her heart so kind, you were quite safe in introducing her into any class of society. She would be sure to make her way with them" (Howe, 1935: 26). Although her sister's marriage spared her the fate of becoming a governess, Jewsbury still had to find a path for herself.

Becoming more personal in her correspondence with Thomas Carlyle, Jewsbury tells him about her specific situation: her sister's guardianship and death, the recent death of her father, and her difficulty in believing in a future meeting or the concept of the soul. She asks him about his beliefs on the afterlife. He offers condolences on the loss of her father and expresses his belief in the possibility of life after death: "it were not even more wonderful than that we now live" (CLO, 21 October 1840). In response to Jewsbury's concerns about the presence of evil (Rosenmayer, 1970: 61), he suggests that she not worry about the future but spend each day wisely (CLO, 30 November 1840). When she writes seeking to know the purpose of life, he responds: "Our purpose, dear Friend? Our best purpose, so far as I could articulate it, is to be and do what God made us capable of being and doing" (CLO, 15 February 1841). He encourages her to keep working since according to Carlyle's doctrine, all work is ennobling and equally important. Reading between the lines that Jewsbury may have been thinking of marriage, Carlyle calls marriage a "confused lottery" (CLO, 22 February 1841), a suggestion that marriage cannot be the ultimate answer for women, an idea Jewsbury would explore in her writing.

Carlyle was flattered by Jewsbury's attention to his words and intrigued by her intelligence and persistence. He led her thinking towards his own ideas, but also reassured her that there were no simple or easy answers that he could give to her, that she must discover her answers herself. Her correspondence with Carlyle changed her life: she received the comfort of a like-minded person who directed her thoughts in a positive way, and his ideas would continue to influence her throughout her life. In February of 1841, Jewsbury announced she would be travelling to London with her brother and would like to call. She was invited to stay with the Carlyles.

The visit started well: Carlyle described Jewsbury in a letter to his brother John: "Miss Jewsbury, our fair Pilgrimess, ... is one of the most interesting young women I have seen for years. Clear delicate sense and courage looking out of her small sylph figure; – a most heroic-looking damsel" (CLO, 3 March 1841). Almost thirty years old, Jewsbury was small and young looking. Jane Welsh Carlyle stated that she looked like a "boy in petticoats" (CLO, JWC to Jeanne Welsh, [15 June 1845]) and perhaps she did not yet dress with the feminine care she was to adopt in later years. Following her visit to the Carlyles in London, Jewsbury started writing long letters to Welsh Carlyle seeking to solidify their bond. Unlike the letters she had written to Thomas Carlyle, these concern the difference between how men and women love: "We centre in them, they centre in what is exterior and lies without them", Jewsbury wrote: "We shall go on loving, they will go on struggling and toiling, and we are alike mercifully allowed to die – after a while" (15 April 1841, Ireland, 1892: 6–7). She quotes a male friend who talked to her about men's interest in sexual passion as opposed to the purer love of women, since Victorian women were believed not to be subject to sexual desire.

Writing to her husband, Jane Welsh Carlyle complained of Jewsbury: "She is far too anatomical for me" (CLO, 15 April 1841). Jewsbury had hit upon a subject with which Welsh Carlyle was as ill at ease as her husband and had no desire to discuss since Welsh Carlyle had little physical relationship with him. Welsh Carlyle joked to her husband that he had passed by Manchester on his travels and neglected to call on Jewsbury: "She who would have been so inchanted to form any modified arrangement with you, for the time being, which a man so hostile to grandes passions had seen useful to propose!" (CLO, 22 April 1841). The Carlyles laughed at Jewsbury's interest in men at a time when sexual desire was not openly discussed.

Although Welsh Carlyle, like Jewsbury, enjoyed the novels of George Sand (pseudonym of the French woman Amantine-Lucile-Aurore Dupin), Thomas Carlyle objected to an emphasis on passionate love, which he termed "George Sandism", because he thought a belief in the importance of passion was encouraged by the reading of her novels, in which women rejoice in physical passion rather than doing their duty. George Sand not only expressed her ideas of free love in her novels, but also practiced them in her life with her prominent affairs with Frédéric Chopin and Alfred de Musset. Carlyle disapproved of Jewsbury's focus on sexual love and wished her to have another object in life. While the Carlyles seemingly lived without physical passion, Jewsbury hoped to fulfil herself physically as well as intellectually. Carlyle wrote to his wife about Jewsbury:

> I wish she could once get it fairly into her head and heart that neither "woman" nor man nor any kind of creature in this universe was born for the exclusion or even for the chief purpose of falling in love, or being fallen in love with! Good Heavens, it is *one* of the purposes most living creatures are produced for; but except the zoophytes and coral insects of the Pacific ocean, I am acquainted with no creature (except George Sand too, and the Literature of Desperation) with whom it is the one or grand object! That object altogether missed, thwarted, and seized by the Devil, there remain for man, for woman and all creatures (except the zoophyte), a very great number of other objects, over which we will still shew fight against the Devil! Ah me, these are sorry times, these of ours, for a young woman of genius. (CLO, 19 July 1841)

In the above quotation Thomas Carlyle uses the term "woman of genius"[6] lightly but portrays Jewsbury as an unusual woman who may become seduced by the wrong ideas, as exemplified by George Sand. He recognizes the difficulty for the Victorian woman of genius of having been brought up with the idea that she should marry and that love should be the center of her world. Jewsbury had yet to find an outlet for her genius, which she would do when she began writing in earnest. Later in her life, Jewsbury made similar laments to those of Carlyle when recommending books in the *Athenaeum* and to the publisher Bentley and Son; she came to believe that an emphasis on physical love in novels was unhealthy for young women as it led them to follow love no matter the consequences, rather than to seek other objects in life. She termed works based on these principles "French novels" and often found sensation novels (discussed in chapter five) similarly distasteful.

On a subsequent visit to the Carlyles, Jewsbury overstayed her welcome and disrupted life in the Carlyles' home. Thomas Carlyle started avoiding her – he tired of her extremes of sitting at his feet staring up at him or attempting to take an equal role in conversations. Welsh Carlyle complained of Jewsbury's posturing in a letter to her cousin: "her speech is so extremely insincere that I feel in our dialogues always as if we were acting a play – and as we are not to get either money or praise for it and not being myself an amateur of play-acting I prefer considerably good honest *silence* – intellect! Carlyle made a grand mistake when he held this Geraldine up to me as something superlative – she is sharp as a meataxe – but as narrow – there is no *breadth* of character in her and no basis of truth" (CLO, JWC to Jeannie Welsh, 24 February 1843). Jealous of her husband's praise of Jewsbury, Welsh Carlyle's opinion changed. According to Welsh Carlyle, Carlyle's earlier admiration for Jewsbury reversed, even his opinion of her good looks: "Carlyle has come to the conclusion that, 'that girl is an incurable fool – and that it is a *mercy for her she is so ill looking!!*'

(CLO, JWC to Jeanne Welsh, 2 March 1843). No longer attracted to Jewsbury, they do not suppose others will be and thus men will be spared being made miserable by being taken in by her looks and marrying her. They laughed at her attempts to entice Carlyle's older brother, who soon tired of spending money escorting her to the theater. Both Jane and Thomas Carlyle commonly exaggerated for effect in their letters. They were used to their own ways of doing things and annoyed by interruptions to their routine.

From the time Jewsbury began to write in earnest, the philosophy of Thomas Carlyle underscored her thought. Although both of the Carlyles evinced anger at Jewsbury, both of them came to appreciate her worth. A complicated woman who could be emotional and trying, Jewsbury was a sympathetic, steadfast friend. Jewsbury never spoke of Thomas Carlyle without respect, and Jewsbury came to view Welsh Carlyle as "more like a lover than a female friend" ([29 October 1841], Ireland, 1892: 39). At the start of their relationship, Jewsbury found a substitute for her older sister in Welsh Carlyle but this relationship would change over time as Welsh Carlyle became more dependent on Jewsbury.

As a child Jewsbury's horizons had been deliberately limited so her expectations would be decreased; as an adult she expanded her own horizons. Early on, she directed her thoughts inward but with the help of her mentors, she discovered how to build a life and a career, and share her ideas with the world. Maria Jane provided Jewsbury with an example of a woman who forged a career for herself under difficult circumstances, finding inspiration and support from her female friends. As one of their father's friends wrote to him after Maria Jane's death: "It does not often fall to the lot of one man to have *two* such daughters" (Howe, 1935: 17). Although that friend was referring to the sisters' abilities as household managers, how much more unusual to have two daughters who were accomplished writers. Thomas Carlyle had directed Jewsbury's thoughts in a positive direction and had introduced her to literary life in London. Like her sister, Jewsbury had great literary talent and was to enjoy a career as a writer, a difficult undertaking for a young woman.

In order to begin to write Jewsbury had to steel herself against a society that like Robert Southey did not believe literature could be the business of a woman's life (Barker, 1994: 262). Many believed that a public career made a woman hard and unsuitable for traditional female activities. Since the loss of her mother, Jewsbury had feared being "hard and unwomanly" ([6 September 1850], Ireland, 1892: 368). As the Carlyles came to know Jewsbury and she shared more of her ideas with them, Carlyle had come to see her as unattractive, and Welsh Carlyle described her as "sharp" but also as "narrow" as "a meataxe". Although she had been mentored by her sister and Thomas Carlyle, Jewsbury had yet to bring her genius to fruition or to marry. She had not resolved how she would live her life.

CHAPTER 2

The Carlyles and *Zoe*: Discovering the World

> [S]he had always heard her father and Nannette speak of marriage, as the only honourable emancipation for a girl, and the only means by which she could be made partaker of the rights and privileges of a woman. Zoe had thus grown to look forward to being married, much in the same way that a schoolgirl looks forward to the holidays, or to "leaving school for good".
> —Geraldine Jewsbury, *Zoe* (1845 [1989]: 94)

Geraldine Jewsbury explores her ideas about religion and marriage at length in her first novel, *Zoe: The History of Two Lives*, published in 1845. Her approach to the topics was unusual for a Victorian woman, and indeed questioning them at all was unusual. Charles Darwin did not publish *On the Origin of the Species* until 1859, after which religious questions became more commonplace. Victorian women were generally raised like Zoe, expecting to marry and looking forward to the event without a real understanding of what marriage entailed. Early Victorian novels traditionally ended with a marriage, signaling a happy resolution for the heroine. Jewsbury did not go along with the accepted truths of society, the way that things were and had been, but sought to make her readers question the underpinnings of society. With *Zoe*, this exploration of religion and marriage brings to light Jewsbury's feminism, as she reveals the problems of Victorian society.

Zoe follows the lives of a man and a woman, Everhard Burrows and Zoe Cleveland, who come from opposite beginnings in terms of religion and family traditions. Everhard, an unfavoured younger son, is groomed for the priesthood against his wishes. Zoe, the illegitimate daughter of an English officer and a beautiful Greek woman whom he married after Zoe's birth, lives with her uncle, an English clergyman. Both Everhard and Zoe are well-educated but unhappy. Because a young man's family will not allow him to marry an illegitimate woman, Zoe cannot make a traditional marriage. Bored with her life, Zoe marries a friend of her father's, Frances Gifford. Although she is not in love, she naively sees marriage as "emancipation" and a means of gaining "her freedom and a position in society" (1845 [1989]: 94). When Everhard comes to England to head Gifford's college, Everhard and Zoe meet and because of Zoe's influence, he begins to lose his belief in an afterlife. Everhard says about Zoe that she is "far too good for the life she has hitherto led – full of passions and capabilities, which have, as yet, found no outlet" (1845 [1989]: 163).

Although given traditional characteristics of their genders in terms of their appearances, she is beautiful and he is handsome, Zoe is not completely emotional, faithful, and pliant as would be expected of a woman, nor is Everhard completely rational as would be expected in the light of Victorian stereotypes. Indeed, Everhard's name underscores his capacity for sexual passion. During a fire in the Gifford castle in the central scene of the novel, Everhard rescues Zoe, who faints in his arms. He kisses her and then carries her to the altar of the chapel where she wakes up and kisses him, but then says: "Forgive me for letting you betray yourself, it was the last thing you desired to do" (1845 [1989]: 245). Because of Zoe's intellectual arguments against organized religion, Everhard loses his faith, and through his physical presence, he has aroused her sexual feelings. The fire, the culmination of their doubts and symbol of their passions, results in Everhard leaving the church. Zoe can only stay with her husband and children; Zoe and Everhard cannot build a future together because she conforms to the dictates of society and because he stands by his vow of chastity. In the novel questions have been raised, but no ideal solution has been found for doubt and love.

Through Everhard's subsequent career, Jewsbury suggests ways by which a person can do good in the world without being attached to a religious order. Everhard travels to Wales where he functions as a sort of social worker improving the lot of the poor. Forced out by evangelicals who seek to control the behaviour of the locals through fear rather than education and compassion, Everhard finds a stimulating intellectual atmosphere in Germany where men think as he does: "they are indeed blessed, beyond happiness, who have a task given them to do, and who can work, not having their ownselves as the end and centre of their task" (1845 [1989]: 117). He discovers for himself the dictates of Thomas Carlyle, to do the task at hand with all of your heart and mind and to be content with doing your duty rather than seeking personal happiness.

Limited by societal expectation, Zoe pursues neither intellectual nor physical activity and has no ability of finding distracting work for herself. When her husband dies, she seeks emotional solace from another person and becomes entranced by the historical figure, Comte de Mirabeau (featured in Thomas Carlyle's *The French Revolution*, published in 1837). In her relationship with Everhard, Zoe enjoys a spiritual relationship when they are apart while her relationship with Mirabeau is based on the immediate force of physical attraction. Since he is already married, Mirabeau cannot marry her so Zoe must give him up as she will not be his mistress and lose her children. Although she is attracted to his energy and adamant ideas, she cannot give herself over completely to another person. Neither her relationship with Everhard nor with Mirabeau satisfies Zoe, but brought up to anticipate fulfilling herself through marriage, she cannot be happy as an independent woman either. Zoe reflects: "What good has my life done to myself or any one else? What profit has there been in all the intellect and beauty of which I so foolishly and vainly prided myself? When I was a child I used to fancy I would do great things, and now my life has nearly passed away, and I am thus" (1845 [1989]: 409). At the end of the novel, Zoe "was neither insensible nor unthankful for all the blessings of her lot – she went through life with a composed and chastened spirit" (431) and looks forward to when she can rest from her labours. Zoe never finds happiness but lives taking care of her sons, doing her duty as Thomas Carlyle advised. There is only the realization that no one is ever completely happy; as William Makepeace Thackeray wrote at the end of *Vanity Fair* (1847–48): "Which is of us is happy in this world? Which of us has his desire? or, having it, is satisfied?" ([1994]: 689).

Zoe had its inception in a conversation between Jewsbury and Elizabeth Paulet in 1841, recounted in a letter Jewsbury sent to Jane Welsh Carlyle: "If we could but make those walls tell all they have ever seen or heard for the last seven years, they would teach (to women especially) more than they have ever yet been taught yet" (15 June 1841, Ireland, 1892: 17).[1] "Those walls" are the walls of Seaforth, the home of Elizabeth Paulet,[2] not far from Liverpool. While keeping house for her brother near Manchester, Jewsbury made trips to visit Elizabeth Paulet, often at the same time as Welsh Carlyle whom she had introduced to the Paulets. An excellent hostess, Paulet wanted her guests to relax and encouraged them to talk freely about such topics as religion and the position of women. Following her imagining the impact of their conversations on other women, Jewsbury intended the novel to reach women readers, to show women the difficulties they face, and the questions she had written to Thomas Carlyle about, in order to direct women towards alternative ways of thinking about their lives. Jewsbury, Paulet, and Welsh Carlyle agreed to write a collaborative novel. Jewsbury saw this as a means of continuing their friendship even when they were apart, of working together in community.

Years later Welsh Carlyle communicated the origin of the scheme and the aftermath: "Geraldine and Mrs. P. and I were to write *a book* among us in the form of letters. I told them to start it and I would take it up when I saw their scheme – they did send me a screed of MS. which I augured no good of, it was so *stormy* – and so I backed out of my engagement, and then Mrs. P. gave up out of indolence – and Geraldine went on" (CLO, JWC to Jeannie Welsh, 4 March 1850). The word "stormy" is her first reaction to what Welsh Carlyle later termed Jewsbury's "indecency" (CLO, JWC to Jeannie Welsh, 25 December 1842). As a married woman with a famous husband, Welsh Carlyle was particularly afraid of being connected with a novel that portrays improper behaviour. Consequently she took a back seat to the project and advised Jewsbury on the content and publication of the novel. Rather than being based on events that took place within the house, the novel ended up being historical fiction, set in the eighteenth century, and thus not subject to the gossip of the time.

While writing *Zoe*, Jewsbury turned away from the influence of George Sand and towards the philosophy of Thomas Carlyle: happiness cannot come from being sought or through the agency of another person, but can only come from doing one's duty. While the "ordinary" people of simple intelligence and lower expectations can find contentment in marriage as shown by minor characters in the novel, complex people like Everhard and Zoe must be sustained by their knowledge of love for each other rather than any physical fulfillment. In some ways their relationship helps to make them better people, as the best marriages should do. Although Zoe desires the physical passion offered by Mirabeau, she is unwilling to give up her life or her children. One modern commentator, Meredith Cary, writes: "one concludes that a sense of freedom and fulfillment for any individual results not from speculation in isolation but from finding some socially useful task appropriate to his capabilities" (1974: 206). Carlyle's doctrine of work plays out through Jewsbury's characters. Everhard, who teaches, writes, and finds an outlet for his intellect, never satisfies his sexual nature. Zoe's stepdaughter Clotilde, loving a man who marries someone else, likewise represses her sexual desires under a religious vow and is cloistered away from society, but usefully schools the young in their religious beliefs. Zoe, like most of Jewsbury's intelligent and emotional heroines, finds neither physical passion nor intellectual satisfaction.

Although daring in some respects, Jewsbury was constrained by the values of her day. She would not allow her heroine to give in to sexual passion with either Everhard or Mirabeau, as she could not approve behaviour of that kind, or at least Welsh Carlyle could not, as it went against the proper conduct of Victorian women. Although attracted by sexual passion, Jewsbury always foregrounded the importance of duty. Throughout her life she would encourage women to do what was right rather than succumb to passion. Jewsbury could not make religious doubt a major problem for a woman, as it had been for her, since the Victorian woman was the keeper of religion and to have her doubt her religion would be "indecent", as Welsh Carlyle termed it. Consequently, while Zoe acts as Eve and tempts Everhard away from religion, ultimately Everhard is the one who doubts the strictures of formal religion and finds an alternative means of benefitting mankind. Jewsbury claimed to have based Everhard on a real person although his doubts were her own as she explained to her friend Walter Mantell: "the type I took him from was also a Priest & a very kind friend to me – he helped me with a few brave outspoken words of counsel when they were needed & most morally courageous they were considering his position & profession – ... but tho' he stood for the type of the character yet I put *my own* religious botherations into him –" (Dunn, vol. 6, 7 April 1858). Expressing skepticism at all was unusual at the time and had not been examined in a novel until *Zoe*; *Zoe* was to influence novelists who wrote about religious doubt later in the century, including James Anthony Froude in *The Nemesis of Faith* (1849) and Mrs. Humphry Ward in *Robert Elsmere* (1888) (see Wolff, 1977). In addition to questioning belief in the established Christian religions, Jewsbury criticizes the evangelical approach by having the human kindness Everhard performed swept away by an evangelical group. Jewsbury thought in new ways about the behaviour of women and the acceptance of religion but was cautious in putting forth her beliefs openly.

While Jewsbury was writing *Zoe*, Welsh Carlyle remained involved as a reader and worked hard to correct what she described as Jewsbury's lack of a sense of decency. A friend of Welsh Carlyle's recorded in her journal in 1847 how Welsh Carlyle described Jewsbury and how Jewsbury described herself at this time, when Jewsbury was in her early thirties; Welsh Carlyle:

> Talked of her brilliant little friend Zoe (Miss Jewsbury), who declares herself born without any sense of decency: the publishers beg she will be decent, and she has not the slightest objection to be so, but she does not know what it is; she implores Mrs. Carlyle to take any quantity of spotted muslin and clothe her figures for her, for she does not know which are naked. She is a very witty little thing, full of emotions, which overflow on all occasions; her sister, the poetess, tried to bring them into young-ladylike order, and checked her ardent demonstrations of affection in society and elsewhere. The sister died, so did the parents, and this wild creature was thrown on the world, which hurled her back upon herself. (Fox, 1882: 220)

How could Jewsbury be "without any sense of decency"? And what is indecent about the novel? The answers lie with Jewsbury's personality, her beliefs about love and religion, and the strictures of the era. Jewsbury expressed her feelings with ease, and delighted in shocking people when she was young. Revolting against respectability, she wrote to Welsh Carlyle: "After all there is something in 'respectability' that nobody can heartily sympathise with" ([1845], Ireland, 1892: 181). The problem is that respectability, in Podsnapian terms of doing what others do, is boring in life and in fiction. Jewsbury looked beyond the conventions of her time to imagine how people should live their lives.

Jewsbury had been raised unsure of the conventions of how things should be and walked a middle line between wanting to conform and wanting to rebel. Although she was in her thirties when she wrote *Zoe*, Jewsbury had the attributes we now associate with a teenager. Following the death of her father, she spread her wings for the first time and enjoyed her freedom. Like herself, her characters behaved and thought in ways that were out of keeping with the strict rules of the Victorian world. To have them give all for love like the characters in a George Sand novel or to have a female character doubt her religion as Jewsbury herself had would certainly be considered indecent in Victorian society. If a female writer expressed such ideas about love and religion in a novel, readers would associate the behaviours and beliefs of characters with that of the writer. Even such sophisticated readers as the Carlyles referred to Jewsbury as "Zoe" at times, as shown in Caroline Fox's journal entry above. Jewsbury noted in her 1846 essay: "The Present and the Future": "It would be social excommunication to express a doubt of any of the points of accredited morality" (1846b: 1443). Many early reviewers of *Zoe* expressed shock that the author was a woman. Calling *Zoe* an "irreligious or infidel Novel" the reviewer for the *Literary Gazette* wrote: "It is hardly possible to believe it written by a female" ("*Zoe: The History of Two Lives* by Geraldine Jewsbury", 1845: 81). The reviewer for the *Critic* exclaimed: "it would never have been suspected that *Zoe* was written by a woman. Lady novelists are usually known by their keen observation of trivialities" ("*Zoe* by Geraldine

Jewsbury", 1845: 313). At a time when women were expected to be the keepers of religious faith, Jewsbury had stepped outside of the mould. She exposed herself to readers by bringing out ethical questions about the values of Victorian society. *Zoe* stands out as intellectually and emotionally honest in its depiction of men and women, and raises problems and questions. One of the things that Jewsbury does best is to show confusion of thought and emotions that come upon a character at once or in succeeding waves. This complexity of thought can appear indecent as, for example, Zoe and Everhard's sexual passion for each other, followed by their unwillingness to act on those feelings. In typical Victorian fashion, such deep, unsatisfied emotional impact leads to physical illness. Her characters lose consciousness, suffer brain fever, syncope, and debilitating illness.

Jewsbury described putting her own thoughts forward as part of her becoming "hard"; she feared she had stopped being feminine in the proscribed Victorian manner. Throughout her career Jewsbury would be torn between her ideas, her desire to influence the world for the better, and her fear for her reputation. As Clarke points out, Jewsbury had been kept to a straight road by her sister and now Welsh Carlyle played the same role: "With Jane in place as an icon of respectability, absolutely firm and fast in her position, Geraldine's freer movements – her free thinking free writing, free loving – could function within a secure frame" (1990: 169). The "spotted muslin" imposed by Welsh Carlyle allows freedom to the thought of Jewsbury's characters but keeps their actions checked. They are not completely naked, but their unhappiness and desperation survive. Their thoughts and desires are contradictions that cannot be satisfied within the limitations of Victorian society.

Welsh Carlyle read the emerging novel and wrote to her cousin Jeannie Welsh:

> So much power of genius rushing so recklessly into unknown space! Geraldine, in particular, shows herself here a far more

profound and daring speculator than even I had fancied her ... – but they must not publish it: "decency forbids"! (as they write at the street corners) – I do not mean decency in the vulgar sense of the word – even in *that* sense they are not always *decent*! – but then their *indecency* looks so purely *scientific*, and so *essential* for the full development of the story that one cannot, at least I cannot get up a feeling of outraged modesty about it ... but there is an indecency or want of reserve (let us call it) in the spiritual department – and exposure of their whole minds naked as before the fall – without so much as a fig-leaf of conformity remaining – which no respectable public could stand ... (CLO, 25 December 1842)

In Welsh Carlyle's view, Jewsbury's indecency stems mainly from her description of unorthodox religious beliefs. More indecent than physical passion in the Victorian public's view was the character's intellectual flirtation with unorthodox religious beliefs, even without going so far as to advocate atheism. Having found her own beliefs, Jewsbury exposes them to a population still traditionally religious. Welsh Carlyle ultimately threw up her hands: "if she will run about the streets naked it is not I who am her keeper" (CLO, JWC to Jeannie Welsh, 18 January 1843).

Welsh Carlyle wanted the novel to have a smoother surface more in keeping with the times, while Jewsbury declared she did not understand the thought of the times. Welsh Carlyle's other objections to the novel were easier to amend: she found that the first seven chapters were too slow, that "the characters should be made to introduce themselves", that Jewsbury "had a very decided contempt for the ordinary rules of spelling – and but little reverence for those of grammar", and that the novel should be "transcribed on 'sheets of similar size' – with margin and the usual neatnesses –" (CLO, JWC to GEJ, 16 March 1844).

Welsh Carlyle sought order in the thought, the narration, and the physical presentation of the manuscript; Jewsbury was not so tidy but laboured to become so under Welsh Carlyle's direction. With the supervision of Welsh Carlyle, Jewsbury strove to become more conventional, but her emotional and enthuasiastic self would erupt at times, although seemingly with less frequency as she aged. While Jewsbury's sister had been her mentor in her youth, and Thomas Carlyle her mentor in her twenties and thirties, Welsh Carlyle became her mentor while working on *Zoe*.

Welsh Carlyle worked tirelessly at making the publication of *Zoe* possible. When she read the novel in its final form, with material removed that she had objected to, Welsh Carlyle responds positively: "I have all Geraldines M.S. now and by the powers it is a wonderful book! – Decidedly the CLEVEREST englishwomans-book I ever remember to have read" (CLO, JWC to Jeannie Welsh, 15 February 1844). Welsh Carlyle then presented the manuscript to Thomas Carlyle's publishers, Chapman & Hall, with a letter from her husband saying that he had not read it himself but someone unnamed he trusts (his wife) liked it (CLO, JWC to GEJ, 29 February 1844). To her cousin, Jeannie Welsh, Welsh Carlyle explained why she helped Jewsbury:

> what is to come of her [Jewsbury] when she is old – without ties, without purposes, unless she apply herself to this *trade*? And how is she even to have a subsistence otherwise, should her Brother take it into his head to marry? all these considerations have made me very anxious to find a Publisher for her *first book*; ... Their Counsellor as to the publishing of new works whoever he may be – told them that it had 'taken hold of him with a grasp of iron' Think of little Geraldine having a *grasp* like *that* in her! (CLO, 16 March 1844)

Welsh Carlyle was concerned for Jewsbury's personal fate more than for the fate of the novel itself. She was also impressed with being told that Jewsbury had "a grasp of iron" indicating the exciting prospect the reader saw in the novel – it grabbed its readers, as it still does. Fearing for the future of an unmarried woman, Welsh Carlyle saw the novel as Jewsbury's way of becoming independent and earning a living. She was prescient in her fears because Frank Jewsbury was to marry and Jewsbury, having published a successful book, had the means of becoming independent.

Jewsbury had her own worries about the manuscript, starting with the presentation of herself on the title page. At first she did not want her name on the title page as she wrote to her publisher, Edward Chapman: "My own impression is that the name of a Miss anybody, gives no weight to a book" (1 July 1844, Morgan Library). Like many Victorian women, such as the Brontë sisters and George Eliot, Jewsbury wanted to be taken seriously as a writer and not limited to the category of acceptable fiction by women: romantic fiction. At the same time Jewsbury, as a young single woman, did not want her personal reputation to suffer because of the behaviour or beliefs of her characters. She suggested her middle name, Endsor, or a shortening of Geraldine to Gerald as possibilities to disguise her sex and identity (1 July 1844, Morgan Library). However, the novel was published under Jewsbury's own name. Jewsbury also debated the title of the novel with Chapman and she suggested the "Mystery of Life or Zoe what should we live for" or "Zoe, or the waste of life" but states her preference for "Zoe, the history of two lives" (26 October 1844, Morgan Library). Tempted to put her moral into the title to make her meaning clear, Jewsbury settled for a title that points out the completely different expectations placed on men and women.

The most important change requested by her publisher was for Everhard and Zoe to marry at the end. When Jewsbury responded that she had another novel following that pattern, Chapman showed great interest in it, but Jewsbury let the matter drop to focus on *Zoe*: "My desire is to produce a work wh shall take a permanent rank at once and not obtain a mere ephemeral reputation" (12 August 1844, Morgan Library). Jewsbury tread a thin line between producing a novel that was new and noteworthy and a novel that was indecent. She was determined to keep the novel within the bounds of decency as monitored by Welsh Carlyle, but also within the framework of what she thought important and realistic. Jewsbury insisted that although Everhard leaves the Catholic church, he would never renounce his vow of chastity and so would not marry. She could not go against the truth as she saw it. Jewsbury's response that she longed the novel to "take a permanent rank" suggests the importance that she placed on the reception of the novel. Not seeking to write a novel that would make a stir and be quickly forgotten, she desired to write a novel that struggled with the difficulties of life and could lead readers to new ideas and thoughts, in her own time and in the future.

Zoe has not "take[n] a permanent rank" among Victorian novels, yet there is much in the novel that is worthy of being discussed, particularly in regard to the picture of the Victorian woman and the possibilities for her of marriage or work or even happiness. In 1845, when *Zoe* was published, readers were shocked by the examination of religion and by the exploration of passion. Despite its excesses of narrative explanation (what is called telling rather than showing) as well as hysterical paroxysms, *Zoe* still makes compelling reading today. The novel raises basic questions: How should we live our lives? Who do we love and who do we marry? In addition, it examines both skepticism and materialism among Catholics and Protestants and looks at marriage and religion from different angles. The novel reveals the problems of men and women forced into roles by families and society. Zoe marries because of the expectations that are not just put upon her, but which she has come to believe, that marriage will bring her status and freedom and will make her happy. Jewsbury never articulates what was wrong with these assumptions – the reader must see beyond Zoe's limited abilities. Just as Zoe suffers from being illegitimate, through no blame of her own, so she is also limited by the expectations placed on women, by herself as well as the men and women around her.

Everhard at first bows down to the familial expectations made of him by becoming a priest but finally, because of his encounters with Zoe, sees the falseness of his position and seeks a life beyond those limitations. He finds work that satisfies him teaching outside of religion and discovers intellectual freedom and appreciation in Germany not in England. His range of movement and encounters are much larger than Zoe's but he is no happier. What remains pertinent in the novel are discussions, thoughts, and conversations that convey the dilemma of deciding how to live an honest and satisfying life that allows one to contribute to the betterment of the world and to developing one's own mind, emotions, and sense of well-being. As in all of Jewsbury's writings there are wonderful moments of truth, such as this start to one chapter: "Under all the different systems of religion that have guided or misguided the world for the last six thousand years, the Devil has been the grand scapegoat… All the evil that gets committed is laid to his door, and he has, besides, the credit of hindering all the good that has never got done at all. If mankind were not thus one and all victims to the Devil, what an irredeemable set of scoundrels they would be obliged to confess themselves!" (1845: 196). In this statement Jewsbury hints at a belief in atheism, for without the Devil there cannot be a God, but avoids making her speculation other than a possibility. Jewsbury risked her reputation in Victorian society, but was not willing to throw it away.

With the publication of *Zoe*, Jewsbury became better known among intellectual circles in Manchester and in London as well. She continued to live with her brother Frank but she knew she could not live there forever. While Jewsbury had not found a suitable or interested man to marry, she had found a means of utilizing her intellect and emotions; Zoe found a man to marry but had no outlet for her "passions and capabilities". Jewsbury was sought after, both by people wanting to know her and befriend her, and by publishers who wanted her work. Her life changed in a way that she enjoyed. Although her favourite activity remained speculating with her friends, she had become a writer.

Welsh Carlyle wrote about the changes in Jewsbury following the publication of *Zoe*:

> Geraldine was a much more lively and agreeable person in Company, when I knew her first – *before* her book – than now – but there was hardly a house in London *then*, to which I could have used the freedom of taking her along with me and now because she has put her cleverness into a *book* – above all a book accused of immorality – (quite a new sort of distinction for a young Englishwoman) there is no house I visit at where the people would not *thank* me for giving them a sight of her and an opportunity of *exhibiting* her to their friends. (CLO, JWC to Helen Welsh, 15 June 1847)

Welsh Carlyle had been angry at the disruption to her household when Jewsbury visited and complained of her exaggerated and artificial manners; but after the publication of *Zoe*, Welsh Carlyle claimed Jewsbury was more agreeable before. Welsh Carlyle resented the sudden fuss made over Jewbury by others and her popularity in the houses of the Carlyles' friends. Welsh Carlyle also jokes that *Zoe* may be the means of Jewsbury finding a husband:

> The oddest thing of all is that Geraldine seems to me in the fair way of getting a Husband by it!!! – Robertson in a fit of distraction took to writing her letters of criticism about it which have led him already further than he thought – and she – has taken or is fast taking '*a fit*' to him – and both I can perceive contemplate a *lawful* catastrophe. THERE is encouragement to young ladies to write *improper* books. (CLO, JWC to Jeannie Welsh, 26 February 1845)

This relationship between Jewsbury and John Robertson caused a panicked interchange of letters between Frank Jewsbury and Welsh Carlyle, but ultimately came to naught.

A reviewer of *Zoe*, who was also a personal friend of Jewsbury's, H. F. Chorley, wrote in the *Athenaeum*: "*Zoe* contains matter enough to demand attention, and to indicate an original mind, though it may not ultimately prove the mind of a novelist" (1845: 114). Chorley indicates that Jewsbury has a promising career in front of her, but is not sure what direction she should take. Jewsbury herself was unsure. Following the publication of *Zoe*, Jewsbury explained to Welsh Carlyle: "I am in a much better humour to write [essays] than to hammer at a novel" and contemplates collecting her essays into a volume ([23 February 1846, 8 March 1846], Ireland, 1892: 190, 200). After the strain of writing a novel, Jewsbury completed several shorter works, many of which deal with the issues she had introduced in her novel, publishing several essays and a short story with *Douglas Jerrold's Shilling Magazine*. In "To-Day" (1846a) Jewsbury calls for a new kind of faith to bind people together, a recognition that Christianity is not enough, a concept she explored in *Zoe*. The essay begins: "The most striking feature in the present day (far more than that of railways even) is the utter chaos into which all previously received principles and opinions are reduced" (1846a: 223). Like many of her era, Jewsbury saw that the Victorian era was ushering in all manner of change and indeed in her thoughts and writings she was part of that change for women and a voice for the reexamination of social classes.

These essays also partake of the ideas of Thomas Carlyle and present moral instruction. In *Past and Present* (1843) Carlyle had bewailed the current lack of connection between people, particularly between those of different social classes such as employer and employee. In "Social Barbarisms" (1846c) Jewsbury examines the relationships between servants and employers, a situation that she believes must change as the employers need to have fellow feeling for their employees: "We have no slaves, – our servants are free; but the actual freedom consists in having nobody bound to care for them, – no one moved to do so by interest, and no humanity to supply the place of it" (1846c: 467). Jewsbury addresses the lack of empathy and understanding common to employers. She may have been inspired to write this article from her experience with placing two sisters as servants, a task undertaken at the bequest of Welsh Carlyle. In the "The Lower Orders" (1847c) and "Civilisation of the 'Lower Orders'" (1847d) Jewsbury criticizes the exclusionary nature of society; for example, she considers the importance of Mechanics' Institutes but believes that what the people are given there is limited, that they should be inspired rather than taught. Adapting the idea of the social work Everhard performed in Wales to present day England, Jewsbury suggests how mankind could be educated and improved through education.

In a short story, "How Agnes Worral Was Taught to Be Respectable" (1847a, b), Jewsbury explores the sad tale of a young woman left under the care of unfeeling relatives who marry her off to a man who nauseates her. Educated without a guiding moral principle, Agnes becomes a governess and is accused of flirting too much with an inappropriate man, inappropriate because engaged to someone else. In *Zoe*, Jewsbury had explored Zoe's marriage to Gifford, a marriage to a kind man but without love that leaves her unsatisfied. With Agnes Worral, Jewsbury describes how a romantic, naïve girl without options is forced to marry, but the story ends just after the ceremony – she does not describe their married life. Agnes "sells herself, in the coarsest and most absolute sense of the term she makes a *better bargain* than the poor wretch who stands in the street at night – the law guarantees its fulfilment, and society agrees to sanction it – but the deep, burning degradation of the REALITY is the same in both" (1847b: 266). Jewsbury makes explicit the analogy between the marriage market and prostitution before Florence Nightingale does in *Cassandra*

(1852). Jewsbury explored the difficulties of education, work, and marriage that faced the Victorian woman in her subsequent works of fiction. Often her heroines have the energy and desires that Jewsbury herself had, but are unable to find a suitable means of using them.

With *Zoe* Jewsbury described the discontent of women but did not present an answer as to how a woman can live a useful and happy life. Before writing *Zoe*, Jewsbury had read extensively, published essays, and done some translation work. With her novel *Zoe*, Jewsbury's feminist beliefs found expression for the first time. She showed how women are trapped by the expectations of their society and unable to fulfil themselves. While Everhard feels hampered by the strictures of his religion and is able to find another path, Zoe remains limited by the marital and societal obligations forced on women. Jewsbury was asking questions about the strictures of society and bringing them to the attention of her readers. Following the publication of *Zoe*, Jewsbury continued to write and undertook to write in many different arenas, both fictional and non-fictional. Jewsbury's creative "genius" stemmed from her energy and curiosity. Her literary endeavours forced her to deal with publishers, to develop manifold relationships, and to become independent. She had discovered a direction for her life. Although she still hoped to marry, she had initiated a means of supporting herself, her own way of enjoying the "rights and privileges of a woman". In all that she did, Jewsbury was setting an example in her works and in her life for other women in alignment with feminist ideas. Through the work they did on *Zoe*, Jewsbury and Welsh Carlyle developed a relationship that would move from one of mentorship to one of equals. In her essays Jewsbury examined the difficulties of class in Victorian society and proferred answers to the problems she saw. She attempted to aid those people, particularly women and members of the lower classes, who held a tenuous position in Victorian society. Jewsbury had embarked on a feminist life.

CHAPTER 3

Fiction and Short Pieces: Educating Readers

> [Women] are crushed down under so many generations of arbitrary rules for the regulation of their manners and conversation; they are from the cradle embedded in such a composite of fictitiously-tinted virtues, and artificial qualities, that even the best and strongest amongst them are not conscious that the physiology of their minds is as warped by the traditions of feminine decorum, as that of their persons is by the stiff corsets which, until very recently, were *de rigueur* for preventing them "growing out of shape".
> —Geraldine Jewsbury, *The Half Sisters* (1848 [1994]: 160)

After the publication of *Zoe* in 1845, Jewsbury continued to create fictional women faced with the problems she saw women confronting in Victorian society. She believed women were as limited by society as by their corsets and wanted to encourage women to question the underpinnings of their beliefs and to find better principles to guide them. All women, she believed, could do something of value in the world by harnessing their energy and applying it to a proper object. Following the publication of *Zoe*, Jewsbury wrote five more novels for adults, two novels for children, and many articles and short stories for periodicals. Through her works she hoped to engage and encourage a new generation of women who could change society.

At the same time that she was trying to open the minds of her readers, Jewsbury felt that she herself was changing – that her writing was making her "hard and unwomanly" ([6 September 1850], Ireland, 1892: 368) and consequently unmarriageable. Although Jewsbury herself did not wear confining corsets, she continued to be hemmed in by the traditional constraints of Victorian society. She could observe society logically but its strictures were part of her upbringing, they could never be completely discarded. By committing her words to paper and having them published, Jewsbury exposed her thoughts, her ideas, and her innermost being to the world. Giuseppe Mazzini, an Italian revolutionary and writer for whom Jewsbury had done translations of his articles, including one on Dante and one on his criticism of Carlyle's view of history, admired the boldness and cleverness of *Zoe*, but he told Welsh Carlyle that he disliked: "its want of *womanness* – 'it is the book of what shall I say – a *man* upon *my* honour!'" (CLO, JWC to Jeannie Welsh, 6 February 1845). Mazzini saw the questioning of religion and the role of women in the novel, the thinking outside of tradition, to be a male trait. Jewsbury was judged harshly by the women and men who knew her best, including herself. By dealing with editors, publishers, and book dealers she showed herself to be a woman of business. These actions removed her from the private sphere traditionally allocated to women in the Victorian era and thrust her into the public sphere inhabited by men. The women she sought to reach with her fiction were not professional women, but those middle-class women who inhabited the private sphere and who expected to marry.

In all of her fiction Jewsbury examines conventional attitudes on education and marriage. Meredith Cary writes that Jewsbury's novels trace "the ill effects of the dependency of women, of their lack of recognition, their lack of freedom, the 'deliberate sensuality' of the training which replaced education for them" (1974: 201). Through her fiction Jewsbury seeks better education for women, adequate means of employment for women, and a makeover of the marriage market, including the acceptance of single women rather than the insistence that all women marry. She encourages women to find guiding principles for their lives, to seek out proper mentors, to take responsibility for their lives, to find a community for themselves, and to become independent or dependent on a suitable person.

The Half Sisters (1848) is the only one of Jewsbury's novels that has a professional woman of genius as a heroine. Yet Jewsbury stops short of allowing her heroine to enjoy both marriage and an artistic career. The novel concerns two half sisters from different cultures who have some similarities in that each is born with some genius by nature.[1] Bianca Pazzi is forced by the sickness and the death of her Italian mother, and her solitary position in the world when she gets to England, to work in order to support herself. She does not choose her profession but slowly works her way up. Eventually she becomes a great actress but never does so out of ambition for her own success, which would have rendered her unwomanly according to Jewsbury. Her ambition is born of necessity and develops into an homage to the art of acting itself due to the influence of an older actor who mentors her. To have to work for one's money becomes an advantage in that Bianca must attempt to put herself forward and to do her best in the work force, thereby fulfilling the requisites of her genius. In a way this was true of Jewsbury herself, who needed to work or to be dependent on her brothers. Genius must be harnessed to be useful according to Jewsbury, it must be secured upon a foundation of moral beliefs that can only be provided by an appropriate education through schooling and mentors, and then exercised and trained to one's advantage. She believed women without genius must have their minds educated upon a secure moral foundation and in a manner appropriate to their class and future.

The other half-sister, Alice Helmsby, has been ground down as she is raised by her mother to be a wife: "She had the sensibility of genius without its creative power; she had not force enough to break through the rough husk of her actual life and assert her inner soul; she had not the gift of utterance in any way, and the life was almost choked out of her by the rank, over-fed, material prosperity which surrounded her" (1848 [1994]: 42). When she spends too much time on her books rather than sewing, her mother tells her: "Your life will be domestic; you are neither to be a fashionable woman nor an authoress; therefore your excessive devotion to books and accomplishments will bring no useful results, but only unfit you for your duties, and fill your mind with fancies" (1848: 14). This advice to a young woman to tone down her desires as she will only meet disappointment, sounds like the advice of Robert Southey to Charlotte Brontë quoted in chapter 1. Alice marries John Bryant but then because he neglects her to focus on his business, she feels bored and unloved. Lord Melton, who often speaks for the author in the novel, describes the problem with women such as Alice: "If [women] are in private life, all their energy is flung back upon them; it becomes overlaid with *ennui*, and they sink into apparent indolence and quietness, but a diseased action goes on within – they are restless, discontented, having so much more energy than they can employ" (1848 [1994]: 220). Like many wives, Alice depends on her husband for her enjoyment of life and all mental stimulation, while he is primarily concerned with his work. Alice's situation is much like that of Jewsbury's friend Jane Welsh Carlyle, who in the early years of her marriage lived in a remote area of Scotland, dependent on a husband intent on forging a career for himself.

Most middle-class women in Jewsbury's fiction are brought up to marry and yet the vast majority of Jewsbury's male characters make poor prospects as husbands. Both Bianca and Alice fall in love with Conrad Percy, a flashy young man with nothing to recommend him except charm. Although he loves Bianca first, Conrad turns from Bianca because "He had become thoroughly disgusted with all that was theatrical, or had a tinge of display in women" (1848 [1994]: 178). As Conrad continues, his words reveal a common belief in society that equated actresses with prostitutes:

> Of late years I have got a real horror of professional women. I never would marry an *artiste* of any grade. A woman who makes her mind public, or exhibits herself in any way, no matter how it may be dignified by the title of art, seems to me little better than a woman of a nameless class. I am more jealous of the mind than of the body; and, to me, there is something revolting in the notion of a woman who professes to love and belong to you alone, going and printing the secrets of her inmost heart, the most sacred workings of her soul, for the benefit of all who can pay for them. (1848 [1994]: 214)

Many Victorian men considered women who exposed their bodies or their minds to the public through their professions as impure because they shared their ideas and emotions with many men.

Conrad fancies a more traditional relationship where a woman would solely reveal herself to him. His ideal woman would be a "relative" creature, not existing on her own, but in relation to her husband or family, and so dependent on him:

> a rational, though inferior intelligence, to understand me and help me in my pursuits; clinging to me for help, looking to me for guidance; a gentle, graceful timidity keeping down all display of her talents, a sense of propriety keeping her from all eccentric originality, either of thought or deed, her purity and delicacy of mind keeping her from all evil, rather as a matter of exquisite taste, than from any idea of the coarse

realities of things, right and wrong. (1848 [1994]: 217–18)

This woman would have no concept of the reality of life because of her sheltered existence. Conrad finds his ideal woman in Alice, even though she is married. Because of her boredom and feelings of neglect from her husband, Alice makes plans to run off with Conrad. When her husband comes home unexpectedly, she faints, confesses all, and dies.

Bianca survives the desertion of Conrad through recourse to her profession and realization of his lack of worth. Eventually Bianca marries Lord Melton, a member of the aristocracy who shows an advanced and open, feminist perspective on women. As a man with wealth and position he is above the opinions of society and can defy its tenets. Lord Melton argues that women are beings in their own right: "Women have an inner life as real as that of man, as full of struggles and griefs; if they are to be kept from evil, they must have as strong a law of right and wrong to control them ... there is only ONE law of what is really right, for men or for women". Although he states he is unsure about the "rights of women" in terms of a woman becoming a "soldier, or a lawyer, or a member of Parliament", he does believe all women should have the right "not to have their lives and souls frittered into a shape to meet the notion of a 'truly feminine character', but to be allowed to grow up freely, and to have their natural characters developed as God made them" (1848 [1994]: 222). His views accord with those of Jewsbury.

Lord Melton would like to see the women of England sent on a retreat to consider "what it is they have been taught all their lives, how much of it they really believe, and how much of it they have ever practiced; they should have to consider what is a real matter of conscience, and what only a matter of convention" (1848 [1994]: 250–51). His plans resembles the consciousness-raising sessions popular with feminists in the 1960s and '70s. By having time to think and talk with each other, they would become "sincere with themselves" and their spirits would be changed. This grappling with the assumptions of education and society was the kind of exercise Jewsbury encouraged her readers to achieve. Like Bianca who was mentored by an older actor and ends up mentoring a younger music student, Jewsbury was mentored by Carlyle and attempted "to refine and cultivate" (Jewsbury, 1848 [1994]: 215) those she came in contact with as a reader or in person.

After her marriage to Lord Merton, Bianca gives up acting when her sister-in-law, Lady Vernon, says to her: "My dear Bianca will not, I am sure, refuse the first request made by her sister; which is that she will not again appear on the stage, now that she belongs to us" (1848 [1994]: 389). A woman belongs to her husband and to her family and her actions could bring negative reaction on that family. Although the modern reader regrets that Bianca cannot have her marriage and a career, Jewsbury provides an alternative that allows Bianca to contribute her talents towards the education of another generation of women. Bianca and Lady Vernon run a school for girls "born in a more pretentious sphere of life, in the odour of gentility, but without sufficient means to get a thorough education" (1848 [1994]: 237). Lewis C. Roberts notes that "Jewsbury does not present this as either a rejection of middle-class domesticity or a privileging of professional careers for women. Instead, Bianca's goal, inherited directly from Lady Vernon, is to inculcate certain domestic virtues in these young girls that will not only make them financially self-sufficient, but ultimately more marriageable, better domestic managers" (2005: 407). Among the girls under Lady Vernon's care, only one has genius, and she pursues her talent. The other girls are of the "shabby gentility". They aspire to a higher situation in life than they have been born into; they must become independent or marry. This class of women dominate Jewsbury's later works of fiction. The independent woman of genius, like Bianca, will survive and triumph; Jewsbury addresses her fiction to women like Alice and the schoolgirls who have unrealized potential and need guidance.

As she had with *Zoe*, Jane Welsh Carlyle found *The Half Sisters* indecent. She wrote to their friend John Forster: "More *actresses*! More 'hysterical seizures'! more of 'all that sort of thing' which played the deuce with her last book! But what can you or I help it since as herself said of herself long ago, she 'has absolutely no *sense* of decency.' What I regret more than the *questionability* of these chapters is the total want of common sense" (CLO, 15 January 1848). Welsh Carlyle may have been particularly wary of the novel as Jewsbury intended to dedicate it to her. She resisted the honour, perhaps fearing that she would be identified with the character of Alice Percy. Few other readers had such strong reservations about the novel. *The Half Sisters* was more popular than *Zoe* and it was Jewsbury's own favourite novel.

Jewsbury never again created a heroine as intellectual as Zoe or as talented as Bianca. With these women Jewsbury invested her heroines with her own intelligence, energy, and creativity. Following her first two novels, Jewsbury's works cannot be accused of indecency, but the heroines are lacking in the spark necessary to envision a life for themselves outside of the societal restraints of the Victorian era. Since Zoe was half-Greek and Bianca was half-Italian and both were born outside of wedlock, their grounding was unusual, and they were able to see beyond the boundaries of English mores while being forced by their situations to conform to society. Dealing with women without genius or with unrealized genius, Jewsbury becomes more focused on changing the individual woman to be able to survive and even to flourish within the confines of Victorian society.

Marian Withers, originally serialized in 1850 in the *Manchester Examiner and Times*, was revised, lengthened, and re-published in 1851 by Colburn in the traditional three-volume format. The novel employs Jewsury's knowledge of manufacturing in Manchester, yet the relationships between managers and labourers becomes only a minor plot. Her main theme concerns the importance of a correct education for women and the horrors of the marriage market. Jewsbury introduces a spinster in her novel, Marian's aunt Alice Withers, who misses out on marrying the man she loves, but lives a useful and honest life and acts as a wise mentor to her niece. The primary focus of the novel is on Marian Withers, whose mind is cultivated by an older man who then marries her.

Like all of the heroines in Jewsbury's novels after Bianca in *The Half Sisters*, Marian Withers desires a lifestyle and a husband outside of her own class and eventually learns self-control. Visiting her richer school friend, Hilda, Marian wants to be part of the life she witnesses and not that which she was born into. Marian falls in love with Albert Gordon, a more sophisticated version of Conrad Percy from the *The Half Sisters*. Albert has been raised and educated without discipline and believes himself above his job as a clerk, which leads to his losing the job. Although he flirts with Marian, he is distracted by a sophisticated, married woman of a higher class and Marian pines for him. Mr. Cunningham, a friend of her father's, tells Marian that a woman cannot live for love, but needs self-control, self-discipline, and to know and fulfil her duties. In this, he is in accord with the teachings of Thomas Carlyle. Following this talk, Marian strives to become a better person in order to marry a worthy man, although she never considers that could be Mr. Cunningham himself. Towards the end of the novel, when nothing has worked out for Albert, he proposes to Marian. By this point, she sees through his superficiality, and soon afterwards accepts the proposal of Mr. Cunningham and marries him. Marian's successful marriage is contrasted with that of her school friend Hilda, who is encouraged by her sister to marry an older, rich ex-roué whom she finds repulsive. Hilda hesitates, but accepts the match. As in her earlier story, "Agnes Worral", Jewsbury compares the marriage to prostitution. Marian, on the other hand, eventually finds a pleasant and proper place for herself in society through studying the example of her aunt and the words of Mr. Cunningham.

Jewsbury wrote to Welsh Carlyle that she planned to keep clear of scandal ([12 January 1849], Ireland, 1892: 280), and Welsh Carlyle approved that *Marian Withers* has "no '*George Sandism*' in it at all indeed, Geraldine is in the fair way to become one of the most moral 'Women of England' Seriously she had made an immense progress in common sense and common decency with the last year" (CLO, JWC to John Carlyle; late January 1850). Something had changed in Jewsbury's writing. After her first two novels, Jewsbury no longer created heroines who were attracted by passion as her earlier heroines had been; in all of her fiction, reviews, and reports following *The Half Sisters*, Jewsbury speaks out against the idea that love should be the most important thing in a woman's life. She refers to novels in which passion reigns supreme as "French novels", and admired and created heroines who "endur[e] to the end" (BA, Reel 47, 2 December 1864). Jewsbury had written two enthusiastic reviews of George Sand's books for the *People's Journal* in 1847 and 1848, yet as she matured, she began to worry about the influence that Sand had on younger readers.

As Welsh Carlyle suggested, Jewsbury's message to her readers does bear some similarities to that of Sarah Stickney Ellis's in *The Women of England* (1839), who called upon English middle-class women of leisure to become accountable for their situation through their own actions. However, Jewsbury does not exhort women to make "their own personal exertions conducive to the great end of promoting the happiness of those around them" (Ellis, 1839: 21–22), doing everything in their power to foster the spirituality, comfort, and well-being of their husbands and family. Nor does Jewsbury evince the Christian overlay of Ellis where all is done in order to secure a place for them in heaven, nor the sentimental appeal stemming from the thought that things were better in earlier times. Welsh Carlyle approved the lack of controversy evident in *Marian Withers*, but Jewsbury's heroine lacks the access to intellectual ideas presented in the earlier novels through reading and conversation.

Continuing her interest in the mistreatment of children, Jewsbury focused her first novel for children, *The History of an Adopted Child* (1853), on adoption, which at the time consisted of taking on a child, often with the approval of the guardian, but without official sanction. Although written for female young adults, the novel's complicated plot extends over three hundred pages. *The History of an Adopted Child* has many of the same themes as her adult novels, such as the importance of education and marriage according to your place in life, but Jewsbury stresses the benefits of traditional religion. The heroine must learn to get on in life based on her capacity and merits. While the novel follows the growth of one girl to maturity, Jewsbury emphasizes the broader aspects of interaction with humanity, such as learning to be kind to others and acting independently when necessary.

The Preface describes the slights that children feel: "I do not think that children are so happy as it is the fashion to represent them" (1853: v). Jewsbury directs her comments to caregivers other than mothers, as her own mother died when she was six and she was cared for primarily by her elder sister and servants:

> It is not MOTHERS who need to be told this, but I recollect so well all my own unhappiness, living as I mostly did, during my childhood and early girlhood, amongst people "who were not fond of children", that I have written this history; partly in the hope that grown-up aunts and elder sisters – when they are tempted to be out of patience 'with those tiresome little ones,' – may exercise some forbearance, and not bid them "go away and play in the nursery, and make no noise". (1853: vi)

This is Jewsbury's only novel written in the first person. Because of the personal voice, the similarity of the child's feelings to her own as a child, and the dedication to Mrs. Darby, Jewsbury's teacher, the novel seems invested with Jewsbury's own emotions.

In *The History of an Adopted Child*, Clarissa Donnelly, who is raised by her grandparents, feels unloved and in the way until her mother, Gertrude, returns from Africa with her husband. Gertrude had hurriedly married a man she "knew nothing about, and cared for as little, for the sake of getting away from home, and the hope of entering a somewhat higher grade of society" (Jewsbury, 1853: 61). Clarissa, just like her mother before her, wants to rise above her station in life and has associated with girls of a higher class during her schooling. She believes that marriage will save her from the life she has and introduce her to a better life in a higher class. Most of Jewsbury's heroines marry in order to escape an "ordinary" or boring future and then find that life with their husband is worse than their single life.

How can women avoid marrying in order to escape from their situations? Jewsbury suggests in her fiction that their home life can be improved, first, by being more appreciated by their family who should not raise them to feel part of a higher class than they are born into. Second, through an appropriate education to prepare them for a future alternative to marriage. And third, by having a more honest perspective of what marriage entails. The self-defeating attitude of some people of high station without money is apparent from the situation of the Donnelly family members who are related to Irish royalty and believe that doing any work themselves reduces them from their proper level. For example, although their house is filthy, Clarissa's desire to clean is attributed to the "bad drop that was in [her]" (1853: 250): namely her mother's blood. The Donnellys believe that people of a higher class cannot work at anything degrading and so do nothing to improve their situation. They are not educated for white-collar work, yet will do nothing else. Clarissa, born in a lower class, makes her position worse by marriage and even worse by trying to escape the consequences of her marriage.

Once Clarissa accepts her lower station in life, she finds

happiness. Becoming a maid for a single lady with infirmities for a small salary, Clarissa performs her job competently. The wise spinster character, her mistress Miss Airlie: "had the faculty of taking, as it were, possession of one, and exciting an intense sympathy and affection in all on whom she chose to exercise her power" (1853: 349).[2] This role of mentor became more important in Jewsbury's novels as she aged and it was a role that she herself would come to occupy. Miss Airlie was the earliest friend of Clarissa's mother and Gertrude was to be companion to her. Gertrude escaped this destiny by ill-advisedly eloping with a man, so Clarissa does the work her mother would have done. Although Gertrude suffered much unhappiness and caused suffering to Clarissa, Clarissa comes right at the end, reflecting on her situation and making a universal lesson from the ideas of Thomas Carlyle: "I do not know that it is wise to talk much about happiness, but the nearest approach to it that I can imagine, is to have work suited to our capacity, and to arise every morning with the definite duties of the day marked out before us, without questioning or seeking" (1853: 347). Eventually, Clarissa meets a man who will make an appropriate husband. At the end of the novel, the threads are neatly tied up with a happy ending befitting a novel for younger people. Everyone Clarissa loves ends up living near her and she and her husband live in the grandparents' house where the story began, fulfilling a need for community.

Jewsbury's second children's book, *Angelo, or the Pine Forest in the Alps* (1855a), less sophisticated than her first and aimed at a younger audience, is Jewsbury's only novel with a male hero and no heroine. The moral concerns the need for patience and religion and living honourably. Adopted by several different people, some good and some evil, Angelo Spara looks to his angel and to God without despairing. Eventually he becomes a famous and rich painter and locates a relative so that he learns about his family, but he never forgets those who were kind to him. In order to make life better for those without resources, he builds orphanages for children where he can, improving the lot of members of the next generation. Jewsbury makes clear the need for kind treatment and proper education for all children. The legacy to the next generation continued to be of prime importance to Jewsbury and something she was aware of in her writing and her life.

Constance Herbert, published in 1855, involves the problems of inherited insanity and the need for doing one's duty despite the unhappiness that may cause. Many of the subplots contained within the novel bring out these themes in different ways. For example, Constance's aunt consents to a Catholic marriage that was not legal in England. She tells her fiancé: "I shall be in your power – if you ever cease to love me, you can be free" (1855b: vol. 2, 215). She sacrifices the security of her future to save her "husband" from a breach with his father that would occur if they legally married, but it exposes her to potential harm. This act, on behalf of love, leaves Constance's aunt vulnerable to the whims of the man she lives with, without legal recourse or societal support. That women should be induced to risk everything for love, whatever the consequences to themselves, continued to be a problematic idea for Jewsbury, and was the basis for her dislike of sensation fiction that became popular in the second half of the 1800s. Constance's aunt remains true to her view of herself as married, while her "husband", who no longer considers himself married when it inconveniences him, suffers a harsher fate.

Constance's first suitor becomes a gambler to ingratiate himself with her father. In Jewsbury's view, a person cannot give up self-respect for love – it is never worthwhile. But there are circumstances in which one must sacrifice one's temporary happiness for a greater good. Constance renounces her fiancé after recognizing the insanity within her family that she might transmit to her children. Eventually three women who have lost their loves, live together and build their own community of support. Constance finds "such companionship and sympathy as she had never dreamed of" (1855b: vol. 3, 13), but this feminist ideal is broken up by the marriage of one and the death of another. For Constance, as for Jewsbury herself, such times were precious and fleeting.

The title of her penultimate novel, *The Sorrows of Gentility* (1856), indicates a theme that arose in *Marian Withers* and *The History of an Adopted Child* – the trappings of false gentility. This is the story of Gertrude Donnelly, the mother of Clarissa Donnelly from *The History of an Adopted Child*. Jewsbury returns to relate in detail the story of a character she introduced previously, providing interlocking stories built around similar themes. The novel begins with Jewsbury's statements on the attempts of those in the middle class to appear like the upper class by mimicking their possessions: "Counterfeits mark a high degree of civilization, and great cultivation of the arts and sciences they represent; but of all the mournful expenditure of human faculty and human energy, the struggles of 'shabby gentility' are the most deplorable" (1856 [1864]: vol. 1, 2). Jewsbury satirizes those people who are not upper-class but who behave as though they are by acquiring the artifacts and trappings of the upper classes (or even inexpensive replicas of them), without regard to true cultivation of the heart and mind.

Gertrude's parents try to buy a life for their daughter above their own, but the plan backfires. Educated at a boarding school among the upper classes, Gertrude gains a superior sense of herself and turns her nose up at her family and her former friends. She works in her parents' inn, but instead of focusing on the task at hand, she daydreams that some young nobleman will pass through and rescue her. While visiting a handicapped friend from school who wants to employ her as a companion, Gertrude meets Augustus Donnelly and runs away with him although she is not drawn to him and knows nothing about him. At sixteen, she just does not want to lead a humdrum life. Written like a moral fable where the characters are basically caricatures, the action and themes are tighter and more coherent than those of Jewsbury's earlier novels.

The reflection of the central themes in the subplots can lead to unrealistic consequences: for example, after Gertrude has been abused by her husband she discovers that several of the women she is close to have been abused by their husbands, an unlikely coincidence. Yet Jewsbury reveals the strength of women aiding other women: Gertrude feels helped and supported by women with a shared experience. The women convince Gertrude that she cannot escape from her situation, but can only try to alleviate her difficulties. Women must take strength from that companionship, but in one's life one must "act up to the sternest requirements that duty claims as right" (1856 [1864]: vol. 3, "L'envoy"), and consequently Gertrude must remain with her husband. Gertrude's greatest trial comes when her husband takes their daughter to Ireland, and does not tell her where they are. Jewsbury ventures beyond satire to show the problems of Victorian society by delving into the horror induced by the legal rights of husbands over their wives and children.

Jewsbury emphasizes the powerlessness of women who have no possessions of their own. They have no control over the fate of their children or even their jewels. When Gertrude admires the diamonds of her mentor, Lady Southend responds with a lesson on value:

> Ah, I dare say you think it would be a fine thing to go to court and wear diamonds, and many a silly girl marries and makes herself miserable for no better reason. If her husband died, the diamonds would go away from her the next minute – (these belong to my son) – and it is paying a heavy price for the hire of them. Nobody would care for wearing them if they went by the satisfaction they felt in it, but they think of the value other people attach to them, and so live in a reflected vanity. (1856 [1864]: vol. 1, 139)

Lady Southend brings to the fore the reality of the law under patriarchy, that everything is owned by men. Lady Southend provides Gertrude with both employment and guidance, advising Gertrude to be honest about her situation to herself, to not look for happiness, but to do her duty. For Jewsbury, women must look to other women for help and guidance, as she did in her own life.

At the end of *The Sorrows of Gentility*, Gertrude nurses her first husband until he dies and then Gertrude marries happily, but the information is tacked on rather than shown. In *The History of an Adopted Child*, which is concerned with some of the same characters as *The Sorrows of Gentility*, Gertrude dies when her child is young, and her child, Clarissa, is adopted by someone staying at the grandparents' inn. Although the events depicted differ, the meaning is the same. Jewsbury's concerns are with the ill effects of a bad education, marriage for the wrong reasons, and the lack of self-control common among young people. Jewsbury suggests, especially in her epigraph from Molière ("*George Dandin vous l'avez voulu*"),[3] that people have only themselves to blame for their difficulties. Even though she clearly sees wrongs in societal expectations and the legal system, she believes that people contribute to their own misfortunes. Consequently, reform begins with the individual.

Right or Wrong (1859b) follows the lives of a man and a woman living in Paris in the previous century. The man, Brother Paul, is a priest like Everhard in *Zoe* (1845), but he does eventually marry. The woman, Marguerite de Méry, is uneducated; she has learned to read but not to write and she has been sheltered to such an extent that she is advised to stay in her rooms so she will not attract the attention of men. A viscount, who can seduce Marguerite no other way, marries her in a fake wedding ceremony. Eventually Marguerite escapes from the viscount and marries Brother Paul. He spends only half of each year with her, and disappears for the other half of the year which he spends in a monastery. Marguerite never questions her husband about where he is for half the year, but submissively accepts his behaviour. The novel, like *Zoe*, explores the suitability of the priesthood and religious commitments for some people. Paul and Marguerite suffer from the conflicting commitments Paul has made to his wife and his religious community. The force of Paul's personality improves the people surrounding him, but he does not function well within the confines of the structured system of a monastery. Marguerite devotes herself to God's will and accepts life as it comes to her, although when her husband is in danger, she does successfully approach the viscount to help them. The novel questions the manner in which the characters depend upon religion, but makes none of its points forcefully. Although Marguerite is too pliable, she appears to have no options because of the limitations of her education and upbringing under strictures more inflexible than those of Victorian England.

All of Jewsbury's novels are enjoyable to read and have a certain charm due to her own intelligence, ideas, and facility of expression. Her novels rely too heavily on backstories for her characters, giving too much information about unimportant characters, telling rather than showing their natures. Other problems involve the pacing of the novels, the contrived plots, and the simplistic characterizations. Few of the characters are subtle, particularly in the later novels. After the early novels, the heroines lose their distinctiveness, and her male characters, with the exception of Lord Melton and Mr. Cunningham, have nothing to recommend them. A review of *The Sorrows of Gentility* in the *Athenaeum* of 31 May 1856 complained of Jewsbury's male characters who are "a brutal savage" or "weak and contemptible": "Cannot Miss Jewsbury conceive a husband who neither beats his wife near fears her tongue? Has she never known a man who is a friend to his wife and a master to his household, ruling in kindliness and strength … ?" (*Athenaeum*, 31 May 1856: 675). The author of this review assumes that husbands are and should be dominant in a household and in society. Jewsbury creates flawed husbands so that she can explore the ways in which their wives survive the abuse or boredom they find in marriage. Through the actions of her heroines, Jewsbury advises her readers, who were mostly women, on their own behaviour and attitudes.

Jewsbury's friend, Dr. R. A. Smith wrote to her on 15 February 1859 praising her novel *Right or Wrong* but saying that he does not believe she has done her best work yet: "– If you were to open up the inner life that you have access to, what treasures would be found – you only turn the key a little bit now and then, because your thoughts are wandering over Combermere & Essex & Huntingdon & Hampshire burying & nursing and forgetting the best and highest duty that you have" (Howe, 1935: 146). This is how Jewsbury's writing feels to us today – filled with remarkable insights and unrealized possibility. Her life was not dedicated to her fiction, but her energy was shared among her novels, her friends, and other writing projects.

During the years she was writing novels, Jewsbury was also writing for periodicals. Charles Dickens approached Jewsbury seeking her work for his journal, *Household Words*. He emphasizes his desire for her "aid" in succinct words, although he acknowledges that he could express himself much more fully: "If I were to write a whole book on the subject I hardly know that I could do more than impress you with a sense of my being in want of your aid, because I estimate its value highly" (Ireland, 1892: xi). Between 1850 and 1859 she published anonymously eighteen articles in *Household Words* of varying length and genre. Some were fiction and more were history, frequently a mixture of genres describing oddities of behaviour, often on the cruel and the unusual side. While depicting other countries and other times, Jewsbury relates people's lives. They contain little speculation, just the facts, and often unusual facts they are. The first published article: "The Young Jew of Tunis" (1850b), contains a moral, to be responsible for your own actions and not to blame others or Providence. Tales such as "Tardy Justice" (1855d), involve cases of mistaken identity; in many of them the person punished for a crime turns out to be innocent. "Specimens of the Alchemists" (1855c) and two subsequent articles on the same subject describe the lives of various alchemists and their inability to tell their secrets to others. She also compiled a short history of early gold and silver mines in England (1856), and the fictional "Nicholas the Rope-Dancer" (1859a) concerning a mistreated child, who ultimately finds happiness. "A Forgotten Celebrity" (1852a) conveys the story of Marie de Jars who desires to be a distinguished woman and who was also an alchemist. This was Jewsbury's first venture into recounting the life of a real woman, a life filled with highs and lows as her fortune varied. For the most part the articles lack a strong authorial voice and tone, but indicate her empathy for people outside of society.

In addition to her works in *Household Words*, Jewsbury published in several other periodicals. With her short fiction, the emphasis is on the need for women to have self-control and the ability to consider their situations rationally. "The Story of Angelique" (1852b), a strange tale, told as true, uses several narrators, an unusual approach for Jewsbury who was trying something new with fiction. Angelique's mother is poorly educated and marries without being prepared. Her husband is kindly, in a similar vein to Mr. Cunningham, Alice's husband in the *The Half Sisters*, but his personality is in stark contrast to that of his wife:

> He a calm, straightforward, and essentially matter-of-fact man, who, having once told her that he loved her more than anything in the world, and reposing in the intense consciousness of his own affection, would as soon have thought of assuring her every day of his existence as of repeating protestations of affection: while she, an undisciplined, passionate creature, with all the mobile, impressionable organization of genius, was constantly made wretched by his undemonstrative, silent habits. (Jewsbury, 1852b: 226)

Angelique's mother has fits of "hysterical prostration" arising from some casual word or slight inattention on his part and her "unregulated sensibility" (1852b: 227). The story ends with death and the suffering of others, the fallout of sin on the undeserving. In a short story, "Agnes Lee", published in 1857, the heroine has self-control and takes a step away from her upbringing in order to make her own destiny. She takes responsibility for her life, without blaming anyone else, which is an ideal for Jewsbury. At the end of her life, Agnes devotes herself to finding out friendless young girls, as she was once, and providing them with employment so they can be self-sufficient. She not only takes care of herself, but like the many of Jewsbury's characters, such as Bianca in *The Half Sisters* and Angelo in her boy's story, she seeks to help others in similar situations.

In 1861 Jewsbury published two "Medieval Sketches" in the *Victoria Regia*, a collection of prose and poetry by popular writers, edited by Adelaide Anne Procter, and dedicated to Queen Victoria. The volumes were prepared to demonstrate the work of the Victoria Press that had been founded by Emily Faithfull for the employment of women in order to show that women could do a job, traditionally done by men, as well as men. To make them more acceptable to the general public, the works in the volume were deliberately not connected with controversial topics (Adelaide Procter to Bessie Rayner Parkes, 7 August 1861). Jewsbury's sketches involve a tournament in the Court of Burgundy around 1440 where everyone behaves exceedingly well. The knights abandon the tournament when needed to fight a war and then fight nobly at the resumed tournament. And yet how strange, how exasperating, that the flower of manhood should consist of these figures who put so much energy, time, and expense into an entertainment or diversion, and that so much admiration be given to them that they became an ideal of courtly behaviour. One longs to know what the women of the time, unmentioned in the sketches, were thinking. Like her articles for *Household Words*, the "Medieval Sketches" would be improved by becoming more than an historical account through some guidance from the author on how to respond to them. Seeking to write what happened, Jewsbury refuses to interpret the events.

Jewsbury persisted in her career, despite her fear that her professionalism was spoiling her as a woman, as Bianca is perceived to be by Conrad Percy in *The Half Sisters*. Jewsbury wrote to Welsh Carlyle: "Whenever a woman gets to be a personage in any shape, it makes her hard and unwomanly in some point or other, and, as I tell you, I am bothered to explain how it is, or why it is, or how it should be otherwise Because, if women chance to have genius, they have it, and must do something with it ... when women are 'incomprise' [misunderstood] they are miserable, but when they are recognized – their specialty spoils them as women, and I cannot at all reconcile the contradictions into anything like a theory" ([6 September 1850], Ireland, 1892: 368). Jewsbury's repeated emphasis on her hardness suggests that she had internalized the Victorian categorizations of men as professional and unemotional, and women as soft, plaint, emotional beings despite fighting the preconceptions of the era in other ways.

Believing that as a woman of genius, she "must do something with it", Jewsbury continued to write and publish, although she desired "a good husband and a dozen children!" ([6 September 1850], Ireland, 1892: 369). Jewsbury wrote to her friend Fanny Lewald-Stahr: "a woman has the best part of her nature underdeveloped until she has children" (GEJ to Lewald-Stahr, Old May Day 1851). Despite her literary success, Jewsbury felt incomplete without a husband and children. The biggest difficulty was in finding a man "of a character and nature large enough, and strong enough, and wise enough to take in them [women of genius] and their genius too, without cutting it down to suit their own crotchets" ([6 September 1850], Ireland, 1892: 369). She acknowledged that an aware, modern woman needed an unusual man. Jewsbury's contradictions, her pull between being a woman of genius and wanting to be a traditional woman, make her human and fascinating, and she was aware that she could not be categorized. Jewsbury cautioned Jane Welsh Carlyle: "Don't try to understand me, I was made to subvert all theory" ([28 February 1846], Ireland, 1892: 191).

While Jewsbury was publishing her life was changing. She moved from Manchester to London in 1854 to be near to Jane Welsh Carlyle, became something of a celebrity within literary circles, and developed many friendships. Although she feared becoming hard and more masculine, she continued to earn her own living as a professional writer. Jewsbury would go on to influence the reading world by encouraging her friends to write and publish, writing book reviews, and reviewing manuscripts for a publisher, helping to establish a cache of books that would, she hoped, benefit the next generation.

CHAPTER 4

Letters: Jane Welsh Carlyle, Walter Mantell, and Other Friendships

> [Y]ou must first have no hope of anything beyond this world, before you can know how very precious is a friend we really love
> —Geraldine Jewsbury to Jane Welsh Carlyle
> (19 April 1841, Ireland, 1892: 11)

Jewsbury asked ethical questions about living a better life in an unjust society in her published writings. In her private life she created relations based on her desire for community, equality, and the need to mentor other people. Her words to Welsh Carlyle show the importance she placed on love for her friends, particularly following her early loss of faith. She did not seek happiness from gaining heaven, but sought what happiness she could on earth through her friendships. Whether at home or when visiting at the houses of other people, Jewsbury spent much time writing letters in order to maintain relationships with absent friends. Among her many correspondents were John Forster, Lady Morgan, Charlotte Cushman, Harriet Martineau, Fanny Lewald-Stahr, Elizabeth Gaskell, John Tyndall, Arthur Hugh Clough, Frances Power Cobb, and John Ruskin. There are three major collections of Jewsbury's letters[1] that show different aspects of her life: with Jane Welsh Carlyle she enters into something that felt to her like marriage; with Walter Mantell, Jewsbury vacillates between a feminine and a masculine role; as an older woman, with Betha Johnes, Jewsbury became a mentor by helping her to become a more aware person who could benefit the future. In her letters Jewsbury reveals an aspect of her feminism closely aligned with feminism today – the breaking of gender and class barriers, concern for the future of women, and the desire for a community of like-minded people who can support one another.

Having lost her mother at a young age and her sister when she was a young adult, Jewsbury suffered from isolation as an adolescent, but developed an emotional and intellectual support system with friends. Letters played a major role throughout Jewsbury's life. Maria Jane Jewsbury's letters to her younger sister and others had formed the idea for her popular work, *Letters to the Young* (1828). Jewsbury's letters to Thomas Carlyle (1840–41) started her friendship with the Carlyles, a friendship that was to last for their entire lives. Jewsbury's first novel, *Zoe* (1845), began as a novel of letters to be written by three friends. But most importantly, Jewsbury recorded her thoughts, ideas, and activities throughout her life and reached out to friends and acquaintances by means of letters. In her letters she records the details of her own life, asks after her friends, seeks to widen her circle of influence and to comfort and support her friends, encouraging them to lead better and happier lives. Jewsbury enjoyed many peer relationships in a society in which women were not the equal of men under the law, and furthered these relationships through her letters.

Her letters provide her with the opportunity to reflect on her life. By using her own experience, Jewsbury provides life lessons for her correspondents much as she makes moral lessons from incidents and characters in her novels, addressing her thoughts toward people she knows rather than unknown readers. These attempts to motivate and buttress, although directed towards the recipients of her letters, are really done for herself: "I am tired to death of writing letters into space; the best of letters are fractions of fragments, and deceive one by pretending to do away with inconveniences of absence – whereas one only writes, after a long separation, to oneself, instead of one's friend. Letters between people who have not seen each other for so long as we have, too, never are the exact signs of the things signified" ([11 June 1844], Ireland, 1892: 128). In her letters, Jewsbury often passes motivation forward; thinking about her friend in Cairo (Charles Lambert, called by her the Egyptian or the "Bey" after his conversion to Islam) and what he has said to her as a good angel, causes her to act as a better person. She writes to Welsh Carlyle: "the certainty that every better sort of impulse that comes to me would be approved of and sympathised with by him gives me a sort of inner life" ([23 February 1846], Ireland, 1892: 187). After receiving a note from Walter Mantell she responds: "Matara you always make me wish to be so much better than I am" (Dunn, vol. 3, 1 September 1857). She attempts to both increase the better impulses of her own nature and to encourage her friends to moral actions. However, for Jewsbury, letters were always inferior to an actual meeting, and she feared being indiscreet in a letter, frequently stating that she has so much to tell her correspondents when they next meet.

The letters themselves are lively, readable, and filled with her feelings of the moment. Jewsbury's words splatter across the page without periods or clear sentence or paragraph delineations. Constant abbreviations reveal her rush. She frequently capitalizes words and underlines them (sometimes more than once), conveying her earnestness and excitement at the moment. She connects her phrases with dashes. Conscious that her spelling and grammar were not conventionally correct, Jewsbury sought help for her limitations,[2] but the letters show no greater regularity over the years. The sheets of paper cannot contain her words: when she comes to the end of her last page and has not yet finished the letter, she frequently goes back to her first page and turns her paper forty-five degrees to crosswrite her final thoughts without adding another sheet.

She attempts to expand her circle of friends and increase the intimacy among them by several means, including the enclosure of a letter from one friend with her own letter to another (avoiding impropriety by asking the sender first for permission). At one point in their correspondence, Walter Mantell requests that she stop sending him letters that he must return. She frequently asks to be remembered to the recipient's family, friends, and servants. Although middle class herself, she was comfortable with members of the upper and lower classes. That she broke the barrier of class and interacted with servants can be seen when Welsh Carlyle writes that her maid stated: "D'ye ken mam I *miss* Miss Jewsbury" (CLO, JWC to GEJ, 12 January 1866). She wrote to her friend Betha Johnes, in between her account of a discussion with the sculptor Thomas Woolner and her description of Henrietta Ward's painting of the little princes in the tower (1861): "I hope you found yr father well when you got back will you offer my best respects & regards to him It was a great pleasure to see you again & I enjoyed our morning together more than I have enjoyed any thing for a long while – How is Charlotte give my love to her – & remember me very kindly to Mrs Phillipe" (7083, 4 and 5 April 1864, National Library of Wales).

Jewsbury's letters often jump from subject to subject, filled with events and places and people, often described with interesting metaphors:

> As for me I have been smothered in the *small coal* of occupations – I read kind[?] MS – I write worse reviews & my life seems eaten up like a cheese by mice – I have been by the sea this summer St Leonards with Ly Combermere & again for a week in Kent with Lady Chatterton – such a lovely old house built by Sir Thomas More & once the

residence of Manport Roper … long turf walks & quaintly trimmed box trees & objects full of lovely flowers – just the garden in wh Milton might have written his Pensees … Mrs Carlyle is greatly better in *all* ways – I have had *no* letter from New Zealand for a great many months. (7087, 15 October 1865, National Library of Wales)

She moves from a description of her life, to her travels, to a quick description of the beautiful home she visited, a mention of Milton, a compliment to the correspondent's talent, news of her great friends Jane Welsh Carlyle and Walter Mantell (well, no news from him). Always, she reminds the recipients to write back: "if only a line" (Dunn, vol. 5, 22 September 1864), to tell her about themselves. Jewsbury does not dwell on her troubles, and spreads good feelings with her messages. There is an upbeat quality to her letters even though through the years, as she ages, she more frequently reports the infirmities and death of her friends. Jewsbury seldom mentions her work (unless writing to her editors) other than vaguely stating that she is busy doing something with a deadline. She almost never reveals her professional struggles or difficulties of any sort.

Jewsbury's complaint about being overwhelmed by small occupations, that her life is nibbled away like "cheese by mice", is a common complaint made by Victorian women. At another time Jewsbury wrote: "This is a long letter all about nothing, but nothings make the sum of female life!" ([10 January 1814], Ireland, 1892: 100). Women's lives were typically taken up with ordering their household, making and receiving visits, and concern for other people. When they had children, the mother was responsible for the early education of all of her children, and often for the entire education of her daughters. Since neither Jewsbury nor Welsh Carlyle had children, Jewsbury urged Welsh Carlyle to write for the sake of other women, as Jewsbury herself did. Although she states that "nothings make the sum of female life", Jewsbury attempted to make something more of her life by leaving a legacy for the future through her writing. Even while publishing her novels, they were never her sole focus as in addition to making money, she was busy keeping up with her friends. Her activities, her interest in other people, gave her pleasure, but perhaps detracted from the intensity she might have brought to her work. As a feminist, Jewsbury broke ground for women in her array of professional and leisurely occupations. She never hesitated to go to lectures or museums by herself or to travel to see her friends. Her letters become about more than the "nothings" of a woman's life, but about how an individual woman coped with the difficulties of Victorian society buttressed by the intimacy of friends.

As shown in chapter two, Jewsbury's most intense relationship was with Jane Welsh Carlyle. They met when Jewsbury came to London in 1841 at the invitation of Thomas Carlyle following her correspondence with him about her religious doubts. He, however, encouraged his wife to pursue a relationship with Jewsbury rather than pursuing the relationship himself. During the period from 1841 to 1852 that Jewsbury continued to live in Manchester keeping house for her brother, she corresponded with Welsh Carlyle. After Jewsbury's brother married, Jewsbury moved to London and lived at 3 Oakley Street, near the Carlyles. Welsh Carlyle wrote to her friend Mary Russell "the most *intimate* friend I have in the whole world ... has decided to come and live near me for good... It will be a real gain to have a woman I like so near" (CLO, 13 July 1854). The correspondence between Jewsbury and Welsh Carlyle basically came to an end when Jewsbury moved to London in 1854.

Welsh Carlyle was the older woman by more than ten years – at the time they met Welsh Carlyle was forty and Jewsbury was twenty-nine. Welsh Carlyle's days revolved around housekeeping, which frequently involved frenzies of cleaning, painting, and ridding the house of bugs, and making his environment such that Thomas Carlyle could write and not be bothered by external problems like crowing cocks or unwanted guests. Welsh Carlyle amplified her adventures into some of the greatest letters of the nineteenth century. Unfortunately, documentation of this relationship is one-sided as Jewsbury destroyed Welsh Carlyle's letters to her (Jewsbury "manfully destroyed" the letters according to Mrs. Alexander Ireland, 1892: xvii) except one. The editor of Jewsbury's letters, Mrs. Alexander Ireland, transcribed and changed them, regularized sentences, capitalizations, and underlinings. More unfortunately, she also substituted words, took out names, omitted sections, and then destroyed the originals of Jewsbury's letters.[3] Even so, the remains clearly show Jewsbury's love for Welsh Carlyle, her capacity to express her ideas and emotions, and her desire for a close relationship of equals.

When their relationship began, Jewsbury swore eternal friendship to Welsh Carlyle, and wrote: "I have found you, and now I wonder how I ever lived without you… I feel to love you more and more every day, and you will laugh, but I feel towards you much more like a lover than a female friend!" ([29 October 1841], Ireland, 1892: 39). Jewsbury follows a common idea of women who swore eternal friendship, but already in the relationship there is a blurring of gender roles. Jewsbury was looking for a man to marry, but felt married to a woman: "For the moment one says, 'I will be your friend,' and you accept it, it is an era quite as notable, and as much to be accounted of as if it were the lover to whom one gave oneself, body and soul, for ever!" ([25 June 1845], Ireland, 1892: 162–63), and "I am writing of myself, for you are mine, and when you suffer I suffer too" ([26 February 1846], Ireland, 1892: 195). Like husband and wife, Jewsbury saw Welsh Carlyle and herself as one flesh – Jewsbury felt a part of Welsh Carlyle's body as well as her life. She wanted to be able to provide what was missing in Welsh Carlyle's life, an alternative to her husband, and in so doing Jewsbury took on a masculine role.

The Victorian era was replete with devoted friendships and yet, as with the relationship between Alfred Tennyson and Arthur Hallam, this relationship feels like more than a friendship. The statements of devotion from Jewsbury's side have led some commentators to think of the couple as lesbians although they were not physically intimate.[4] According to Martha Vicinus: "Their friendship is not a lesbian story, but rather a narrative that makes possible lesbian understandings. It illustrates how a woman who tried and failed to win a husband, who seemed at times too assertively masculine and at others too emotionally feminine, could gain a hold on the affections of a woman who prided herself on her rationality and self-control" (2004: 115). The statement that Jewsbury was both "too assertively masculine" and "too emotionally feminine" shows Jewsbury as outside of the Victorian expectations for a woman. As Jewsbury wrote to Walter Mantell: "I was a human being before I was of the *female* persuasion" (Dunn, vol. 6, January 1858). Jewsbury believed all women should be considered first as rational human beings. In this she follows Wollstonecraft who writes at the start of *A Vindication of the Rights of Woman*, that men often consider "females rather as women than human creatures" (1792 [1967]: 31). In her letters, issues of gender, common among feminists today, appear frequently. Jewsbury crossed the distinctions between men and women made by many Victorians and forged her own gender identity just as she made her own place in Victorian society.

Jewsbury wanted someone intelligent and understanding to provide a steadying force in her life, as a man might provide, and Welsh Carlyle was there at the right time: "I cannot explain to you the superstitious value I set on those I ever love, and the sort of religious feeling with which I try to guard every word or thought which might raise a shade between us" ([19 April 1841], Ireland: 1892, 11). Although she was afraid to "raise a shade" between them, she managed to anger Welsh Carlyle frequently. Welsh Carlyle did not immediately or consistently return the degree of affection that Jewsbury felt towards her. Because of Jewsbury's excesses, her always "dropping hot tears on my hands" (CLO, JWC to Jeannie Welsh, 18 or 19 January 1843) and her "natural superabundance of emotion" (CLO, JWC to Jeannie Welsh, 2 February 1843), Welsh Carlyle was at first reluctant to become close to Jewsbury, even writing that Jewsbury is "'a vile creature'" (CLO, JWC to Jeannie Welsh, 13 April 1843). Welsh Carlyle disliked Jewsbury's interest in men and declined to engage in her conversations about passion. Jewsbury wrote to Welsh Carlyle, by way of apology for an outburst: "You will have no more of those explosions of temper which horrified you so much, and which arose from my not being able to reconcile certain things – from being perplexed between my own fancies and real things" ([23 February 1846], Ireland, 1892: 193). Jewsbury did not carry grudges; she expressed her feelings and moved on. When angry, Welsh Carlyle adopted the silent treatment.

Their relationship always had its ups and downs. In her essay "Geraldine and Jane" (1935), Virginia Wolf describes the scene at Seaforth House, near Liverpool, in July 1844 when both women were staying with their friend, Elizabeth Paulet, where they had a disagreement leading Jewsbury to become jealous and to sulk:

> A few days later [Welsh Carlyle] turned upon Geraldine in public and sent the whole company into fits of laughter by saying: "I wondered she should expect me to behave decently to her after she had for a whole evening been making love before my very face to *another man!*" The trouncing must have been severe, the humiliation painful. But Geraldine was incorrigible. A year later she was again sulking and raging and declaring that she had a right to rage because "she loves me better than all the rest of the world"; and Mrs. Carlyle was getting up and saying: "Geraldine, until you can behave like a gentlewoman …" and leaving the room. And again there were tears and apologies and promises to reform. (1932)

Welsh Carlyle makes a public joke out of a private quarrel by pointing out their unusually gendered relationship. She uses Jewsbury's emotions to amuse the other inhabitants of the house and later her husband by writing an account of the incident. Despite the passionate expression of Jewsbury's emotions, and her public humiliation, Jewsbury's friendship with Welsh Carlyle continued, although it was occasionally interrupted by Welsh Carlyle's silences.

Jewsbury believed, as Thomas Carlyle and his physician brother did, that Welsh Carlyle would have been happier with more of a purpose to her life and suggested she write: "half your loneliness comes from have no outlet for your energies, and no engrossing employment" (6 October 1851, Ireland, 1892: 427). Jewsbury began working on *Zoe* as a means of providing incentive for Welsh Carlyle's writing and as a means of developing their friendship with each other and Elizabeth Paulet. In her letters Jewsbury dwells on the benefits of writing: "I hope you are thinking of our tale. Do make an effort! It will take your thoughts off disagreeable things. I can tell you, from experience, that whilst one is in for writing a tale, it becomes the reality for the time being, and all other things grow shadowy, and I don't think it is one bit more wearing than it is to worry one's self about the things of one's own life" ([1847–48], Ireland, 1892: 240). If Welsh Carlyle was worried that writing fiction would be wearing, Jewsbury reassures her that writing is no more tiring than living and has the advantage of taking one outside of oneself and one's own problems. Jewsbury wrote at another time that when writing "we not only feel less acutely things that would otherwise irritate beyond endurance, but these things are transformed for us into artistic studies, instructions, experiences, and this goes a long way towards softening their intensely personal application to ourselves Besides which, one's work is an 'ark of refuge,' into which one flings oneself on all occasions of provocation" (6 October 1851, Ireland, 1892: 425). While Jewsbury had her work for refuge,

Welsh Carlyle had Jewsbury.

Jewsbury saw something in Welsh Carlyle that others did not always see: she saw beyond the cleverness and attempted to bring out what she considered the "real" Welsh Carlyle. Jewsbury frequently requests that she use less art to tell her how she is – Jewsbury wants to hear about *her*: "I always grudge your writing about news (or) witty letters like the last – I want to hear about you, and there is nothing else you can tell me that I care to hear" ([1843], Ireland, 1892: 72). Jewsbury encouraged Welsh Carlyle to write, showing her a path to make Welsh Carlyle more accepting of her husband because less dependent on him. She believed Jane Welsh Carlyle had much to share with other women: "I think you might have enough maternal feeling, sisterly affection, or what you will to wish to help other women in their very complicated duties and difficulties" (6 October 1851, Ireland, 1892: 426). Jewsbury appealed to Welsh Carlyle to write for her metaphoric daughters, including herself: "I am one of your children, after a fashion" (6 October 1851, Ireland, 1892: 427). Jewsbury feels like her daughter because she has learned from Welsh Carlyle. Although Welsh Carlyle never published for the benefit of others, Jewsbury continued to do so, but changed her emphasis in her writing because of their relationship. Jewsbury valued Welsh Carlyle highly, writing to Walter Mantell: "I am very glad you like *her*. – She is one of those who cannot be judged, but must be accepted she is a heroine – & right or wrong makes a prescription for herself … & as to her *fascination* I appeal to *yrself*." (Dunn, vol. 8, 18 October 1859). Jewsbury terms Welsh Carlyle a "heroine" in her ability to endure her unhappiness without complaint, and she became an ideal for Jewsbury, and the model for several of the characters in her novels.

Ultimately both women received a confirmation of sisterhood from the relationship. Jewsbury perceived a duty among women to support each other, especially those members of the sex without other people, like a sympathetic husband, to support them. Feeling a deep unity with the unhappiness of women, Jewsbury developed a common bond with Welsh Carlyle and sought to recognize their similarities and not their differences. She saw them both as struggling against the limitations of their society, as women who were ahead of their time. They were both unusual women who stood out for their talents but while Jewsbury despaired at being single, Welsh Carlyle suffered because of the nature of her marriage. It is in a letter to Welsh Carlyle that Jewsbury makes her strongest statement of feminist beliefs:

> I believe we are touching on better days, when women will have a genuine, normal life of their own to lead. There, perhaps, will not be so many marriages, and women will be taught not to feel their destiny manqué if they remain single. They will be able to be friends and companions in a way they cannot be now. All the strength of their feelings and thoughts will not run into love; they will be able to associate with men, and make friends of them, without being reduced by their position to see them as lovers or husbands... I do not feel that either you or I are to be called failures. We are indications of a development of womanhood which as yet is not recognized. It has, so far, no ready-made channels to run in, but still we have looked, and tried, and found that the present rules for women will not hold us – that something better and stronger is needed. ([1849?], Ireland, 1892: 347–48)

Jewsbury saw the bond between women as powerful and the future of women as filled with possibilities. She recognized the problem of women at the time as not having "ready-made channels to run in", a lack of foremothers, and consequently they had to blaze their own way in Victorian society. Although women's problems have been deemed minor by the world around them, Jewsbury understood the difficulty of the position of the Victorian woman whether single or married, and had explored both states in her writings. Although she was not openly seeking female emancipation, and even mocked those women who were, Jewsbury felt a kinship to other women. Both Welsh Carlyle and Jewsbury struggled against the difficulties women faced in a patriarchal society and helped each other through their difficulties. Jewsbury saw how women were changing, how men would be changing, and saw herself as part of that process:

> There are women to come after us, who will approach nearer the fullness of the measure of the stature of a woman's nature. I regard myself as a mere faint indication, a rudiment of the idea, of certain higher qualities and possibilities that lie in women, and all the eccentricities and mistakes and miseries and absurdities I have made are only the consequences of an imperfect formation, an immature growth. ([1849?], Ireland, 1892: 348)

Jewsbury understood that she was part of a force of women who took strides forward to work towards change, and could be a foremother for the next generation.

Jewsbury's interest in men was a bone of contention between herself and Welsh Carlyle. Welsh Carlyle stated that Jewsbury was "never happy unless she has a *grand passion* on hand" (CLO, JWC to Mary Russell, [16 Jan. 1858]). Although she always wanted to marry, Jewsbury recognized that it would not happen easily. During the late 1850s, Jewsbury had four major relationships with men: first with a friend of her brother's to whom she became briefly engaged (John Robertson), second with a man only known as Q in the letters, then with Charles Lambert, and finally with Walter Mantell. Welsh Carlyle claims Jewsbury proposed to all four but information on Jewsbury's relationships with the first three is scarce while her letters to Mantell are plentiful.[5]

Jewsbury wrote over five hundred letters to Walter Mantell

(1820–95). Through many of the letters Jewsbury attempted to help Mantell become a better and more productive person by pointing out the positive aspects of his characters and exhorting him to use his abilities to help the Maori people and to be a leader. Mantell had gone to New Zealand at an early age and worked for the government making agreements with the Maori for their land. Learning that the government was not living up to the contracts, he returned to England for three years during which he met Jewsbury and often expressed his anger over the treatment of the Maori. Jewsbury felt sympathy for the Maori following discussions with the former Governor of New Zealand, Sir George Grey, whom she had met with the Carlyles and from discussions she had with Walter Mantell. She pleaded with him to write, and even contacted publishers for him (Dunn, vol. 2, 6 March and 27 May 1857) and urged him to assume a role in public life in New Zealand (see Wilkes, 1988). In their letters she addresses him as "Matara" which means chief, the name given him by the natives of New Zealand who could not pronounce Mantell. As she wished a Maori name, he gave her the name "Manu", meaning bird. He constantly thinks of her as a friend, and refers to her fondly as "dear Manu", but never romantically. At a time when an unmarried woman rarely communicated with a man, Jewsbury behaved outside of convention, but Mantell never seems to have questioned her motives.

Jewsbury was forty-four when they met in 1856, eight years older than Mantell; she was fascinated by him and his experiences. Jewsbury took the lead in their friendship and in trying to turn the relationship into a romance. At first Jewsbury sought to ingratiate herself, to give him a reason to correspond: "I am sure that writing letters to 'an intelligent correspondent' is good for you, so please send me word how you are" (Dunn, vol. 2, 26 January 1857). She became closer with him as time passed by and acknowledged in 1857 that:

> This time last year I was only *wishing* to have you my friend. Now I *have* you & I am so much the richer in my life – dear Matara do not let anything drift us away from each other – hold me very fast & don't ever let me do wrong or be wrong – & [it] is so strange to look back & to *recollect* how I was looking at you last Xmas drawn with instinct to wish to come near you – & how *many* things have grown up & unfolded from that germ! – (Dunn, vol. 3, 25 December 1857)

After knowing him for a year, the relationship which had been one of friendship and equality changes. Feeling close to him, Jewsbury asks Mantell to be responsible for her: "don't ever let me do wrong". She has switched from believing the relationship will be good for him, to wanting it to be beneficial for her. She expects him to control her and seeks to present herself as more traditionally feminine, thus showing a clear interest in a romantic relationship with him. In offering obedience to him, Jewsbury comes close to describing the Victorian ideal of the marriage relationship and again shows her desire for someone to take care of her. As she did with Welsh Carlyle, Jewsbury feels herself so much a part of him that she suffers when he is ill as though their bodies had been joined in marriage (Dunn, vol. 8, 15 September 1859).

Jewsbury emphasized her similarities to Mantell. Like him, Jewsbury worked for a living at an occupation that, for a woman, had few precedents. She wrote to him that her "life for a woman has been as hard as yours for a man & in some things not unlike it". This has led to both of them getting below the surface; "there is the reason why we did not talk on the *outside* of things" (Dunn, vol. 2, 7 April 1857). She seeks in 1857 to convince him of her lack of artifice, her truthfulness, and becomes angry that he has misunderstood her:

> only I entreat you not to call any of my letters "clever" – it is the last worst epithet I CD receive from you – you do not

> know how completely my letters to you are *suggested* by you – I write to no one else as I do to you – it is like breathing – I say what I want to say & certainly being "clever" is the last thing I dream of – Don't you see – oh blind & stupid – *man* that you are! – that what I write out to you is out of my life – that letter that "struck you as so *clever*" was an experience learned with many tears out of a lesson book as sadly torn & degraded that no ones eyes may even see it (Dunn, vol. 3, 1 September 1857)

The incident itself cannot be recovered from the letters but her words and tone in the letter are insulting: "Oh blind & stupid – *man* that you are!" Because she has gone through something similar and learned from it, she attempts to use her experience to guide him. She lauds her sense of superiority in the world of emotions that he cannot comprehend as a man and stands up for the heart in her letter rather than the artifice.

When baited, Jewsbury extols her own worth and forgets that she wants a man to set her on a more traditional path and keep her to it. She stands up for herself in a masculine and forthright manner, at least for a while:

> Lady Combermere asked me to go to her tomorrow & I am going somewhere about half past nine of ten – do you scornfully say "why do you go if you pretend not to care for parties?" I will tell you first, I like to see things & people – as a spectator but as play – it is part of my profession 2nd I generally amuse myself in a placid way (when I am not [damaged?] as I felt last night) & lastly & chiefly because I earned whatever success I may have – without help from anybody – & if one has earned even the right of putting their right foot before the left there is a value in it not its own … I have entered into all this detail because I want *you* to see me right where I am wrong; "vain things cannot profit", &

> I trust in you as a *pierre de touche* [touchstone] – & that you will burn up any vanity or foolishness you see in me … I used to have faith in my own discernment to know good & evil but now I know nothing & every day feel more helpless & the need to be taught. (Dunn, vol. 2, 18 July 1857)

She corrects Mantell's assumptions, but she also asks for his help in setting her straight in the future. At times in their correspondence there is a strong sense of inequality as though Jewsbury found him superior to herself and tries to remake herself – how she writes, how she dresses and how she entertains or talks – in order to please him. When he complains of her statements or behaviour, she responds that she is not perfect and asks him to have patience with her; at other times, she defends her behaviour, showing that she could never give herself over to him completely.

She encourages Mantell to write, to share his knowledge of the Maori and New Zealand: "I want you to write a book about your New Zealand because I want to read it myself – & you will never tell me all I want to know and I know that it WD do you a world of good to write out" (Dunn, vol. 2, 6 January 1857). Jewsbury wrote a review of a book on the treatment of the Maori people but clearly wished she could do more ('*The Maori King*', *Athenaeum*, 1 October 1864: 423–25) and often upbraids Mantell for his anger rather than activity. She gets exasperated by his complaints about the work that others are doing as he does not take action himself:

> you don't care for what YR friends *do* – you are luxurious & like to have what they *are* – the way you ask me about my book is *exasperating* – as you WD find out if ever you wrote one – I don't want you ever to mention it again – certainly I shall never answer you – it is striking 11 o'clock I am not going to sit up any longer making myself look like a *witch* in YR service – I send YR letters back as you desired – please commit no more "pious frauds" on me – as they will

be resented – & *you* will suffer – (Dunn, vol. 3, 1 October 1857)

Jewsbury stings from his having disparaged her writing and displays her annoyance. Mantell responded to Jewsbury's anger, standing up for his behaviour and explaining that he is interested in her writing, but that she will not tell him about it in any kind of real way: "I respect it & more respect & admire you for your courageous pursuit of it… Again & again have I asked you how you were getting on & tried to ask so that you should see how real an interest I took in the answer but you have given none until this last letter tells me that I have only 'exasperated' you & convinced you that I care nothing about the book or the writer. Not fair of you, to say the least" (Dunn, Vol. 1, 6 October 1857). Mantell's complaint, that Jewsbury is "not fair", comes up a few times in their correspondence and suggests his belief that Jewsbury thinks more of herself and her opinion than of him, despite her frequent pronouncements of his superiority. Jewsbury does not adopt the stance of a typical Victorian woman; she takes her professional activities seriously and will not have them made light of by anyone but herself.

Her real criticism of Mantell is that he is not doing anything with his talents while she works diligently, an arrangement which is against the Victorian expectations for men and women. She accuses him of not being productive: "It is a hard thing to say but you are living a life of self-indulgence – I don't mean you live *softly* – I mean that you do nothing you don't feel *inclined* to do – your life has no work of *obligation* in it" (Dunn, vol. 7, [8 March 1859]). Jewsbury may resent that she must work hard to earn her living rather than being dependent on a man as most women were in the Victorian era. Jewsbury's anger was short lived and she did indeed mention her writing again requesting that he improve it by editing. Most of the time Jewsbury treated Mantell with respect and as her superior, but at times she became frustrated because she wanted more for him than he wanted for himself; she wanted him to do something important in the world. As a woman, she had a difficult time in achieving as much as she did. She believed, as a man, he should have used his advantage in a meaningful way.

Although Jewsbury stated that she wanted to marry, her personality was forceful and independent enough to scare away almost any man, especially a husband who sought obedience from his wife. As she began to think of Mantell romantically, Jewsbury advises Mantell that "We [women] desire nothing better than to obey one wiser & stronger than ourselves", and she seems to believe it (Dunn, vol. 2, 10 April 1857). She repeats a similar sentiment expressed by Thomas Carlyle with anger: "a woman's natural object in the world is to *go out* & find herself some sort of *man her superior* – & obey him loyally & lovingly & make herself as much as possible into *a beautiful reflex of him!*" (Dunn, vol. 2, 10 April 1857). Although she is looking for a superior man, Jewsbury does not see that as her main object in life nor should a woman be a "*beautiful reflex*" of a man. Jewsbury continues by stating that the problem is not so much with the woman as the man: "true enough the difficulty is to find a man who *can* be our master … we set up an idol & hope it will rule us like a true god – but when it cannot & does not – we fling it down & break it to pieces to mend the roads withal – it is not women who fail in docility but the men who are not high enough to rule" (Dunn, vol. 2, 10 April 1857). Jewsbury desired to shape Mantell into that man who could rule her but at the same time she rebelled against being ruled. He clearly sought a docile woman and Jewsbury revealed herself to be otherwise despite her statements that she seeks someone to be her master. The unrealistic expectations that Victorian men and women had for each other in marriage were not something that Jewsbury was comfortable with, as she shows in her fiction. During the Victorian era, there seemed no clear path for strong women who wanted to marry strong men they considered superior to themselves. After all, Jewsbury was older than Mantell, she was financially independent, she was well known for her publications, and she was used to being on her own. She was conflicted in her thoughts, imagining a relationship of equals, at the same time as she tried to behave like a Victorian doll.

By praising what she admires in him, she seeks to mould him into the kind of man she wants him to be: "You have that kind of character which imposes respect for all its decisions no matter whether the rescuer be prosperous or not or whether the cause be 'prudent' or not because all who come under your influence know that you are inflexible only in what you think right. You do not regard either gains or losses you are in a region above them so in God's name do not let your serenity be ruffled or mind tormented" (Dunn, vol. 1, dated Monday). And in praising him, she often puts herself down: "I will try to be more gentle & *not* to take any more fancies for realities – but Matara *if* I should – do not be hard with me – recollect how much stronger *you* are than I am" (Dunn, vol. 1, dated Sunday). As with Welsh Carlyle, Jewsbury sometimes belittles herself by imagining herself as weak because she sought to be supported by someone else's strength. She tried to reflect to Mantell the image that she knew would appeal to him, and yet her belief in herself and her accomplishments comes through. Jewsbury recognized that as women became independent, more like today's feminists, new men were needed who would fall in love with them for their strengths and not their weaknesses.

Mantell developed a passion for Calliope Dilberoglue, who was young, beautiful, innocent, and obedient, very different from Jewsbury herself. The family was Greek and so traditional that Mantell approached Calliope's guardian, her brother, for permission to court Calliope. Her brother refused his permission, and Mantell was thrown into a depression. As the time approached that Mantell would return to New Zealand in 1859, Jewsbury evidently proposed to Mantell and the discussion did not go as she wanted. Jewsbury followed up with a letter in which she declared that Mantell let his feelings for her be known by saying he is fond of her. He noted in the margins of her letter that this particular remark is "nonsense" and the more general comment: "A most untruthful & unfair letter" (Dunn, vol. 8, 28 August 1859).

Her letter begins with a reference to a book she is going to send him, a matter of practicality, proceeds to her arguments for marriage, and ends with a melodramatic plea. Her pen runs away with her and she sends him the letter because she wants him to know everything she thinks. Welsh Carlyle had advised Jewsbury from the start of the relationship not to be open with Mantell, but Jewsbury never shied away from expressing herself and believed she could show him herself with all her conflicts. Like the marriage proposals in her novels, her statements to Mantell argue for their compatibility rather than being admissions of passionate love, yet she also reveals her emotional nature and her inability at times to control those emotions, leading to what would have been considered outlandish behaviour. Living alone, Jewsbury was used to getting her own way which she stated was more important than emancipation (Letter to Mr Sydenham Nodes[?], 21 July 1851, William Hepworth Dixon Papers, UCLA). With Mantell, Jewsbury did not get her own way and no changes of laws could help her.

In her letter, Jewsbury gives rational reasons for the anticipated success of their marriage: she has a gift of assimilation, a good temper, and money. Her best argument is un-Victorian: Jewsbury critiques the whole tradition of men proposing to women by stating that the decision should not be one-sided. She desired a marriage of equals, but as she continues to write, Jewsbury moves further and further from rational discourse into passionate desperation. She ends the letter: "Take me away with you or send to fetch me or else – set your foot on my neck & kill me it is neither right nor just to leave me in this misery" (Dunn, vol. 8, 28 August 1859).

In her novels Jewsbury calls for women's self-control, perhaps because she recognized how much her own life was governed by emotion. In her private life she expressed her emotions and broke the Victorian courtship conventions in which women only had the right of acceptance or refusal. Jewsbury vacillated between logic, a traditional characteristic of men, and emotionality, attributed to women, always being honest in the moment, in her deepest relationships, those with Welsh Carlyle and Water Mantell. Although she challenged conventions, she was also trapped by societal expectations, the rules that she was brought up with, which were the rules that governed the Angel in the House. Jewsbury moved back and forth between trying to adapt herself to convention, and acting outside of societal expectations. Jewsbury was uneasy with Victorian gender conventions and could disassociate from them at times with Welsh Carlyle and Mantell.

After Mantel returned to New Zealand, Jewsbury became friendly with the Johnes family living in the Dolaucothy estate in southwest Wales. She wrote letters to members of the family, the daughter Betha in particular, between 1860 until close to Jewsbury's death in 1880. In 1860 the Johnes family consisted of Judge John Johnes (1800–76), a widower since 1848, and his two daughters, Charlotte Johnes Cookman (who had been widowed in 1859) and Elizabeth Johnes (1834–1927; later Lady Hills-Johnes), known as Betha. When this correspondence began, Jewsbury was forty-eight and Betha Johnes was twenty-six. Jewsbury's letters start as advice and are peppered with suggestions for Johnes's reading and attitudes, an attempt to shape the mind of a young person. The letters also describe the relationships, outings, lectures, and events that filled Jewsbury's life, and in that they read like a journal.

When first visiting Dolaucothi, Jewsbury described Bertha Johnes in a letter to Walter Mantell:

> *very* lovely – like a fairy – full of talent sings like an angel – draws like an artist is *clever* in every thing, housekeeping especially – her cleverness only *just* stops short of being genius – she rides like an amazon … She has a lovely Arab steed *pur sang* reddish grey – very gentle & spirited as becomes

> its race, as fleet as the wind, and goes like a bird, and it is one of the prettiest sights I ever saw to see her on horseback when she puts *Llamrei* (the name of King Arthur's horse) to his full speed the plume – of her hat streaming in the wind – & a scarf she wears for warmth – over her shoulder has a charming effect – & she is so good & simple – I am glad I am not a man – for she is very dangerous to their peace of mind! (Dunn, vol. 5, 24 September 1863)

Her description paints a mythic picture. Jewsbury feels admiration and concern for Johnes and praises her for her womanly attributes (her ability to sing and draw and keep house) while also admiring the independence and spirit that allows her to gallop her horse (while still looking beautiful).

The letters are very different from her letters to Carlyle and Mantell in that there is less of her personal feelings and more of a record of her activities. She began as a mentor to Betha, but as Jewsbury aged, Betha and her sister came to assist her by acting as her amanuenses and helping her with errands. Whereas with her letters to Carlyle and Mantell, Jewsbury's honesty and forthrightness shine forth as she expresses her feelings, in her letters to Johnes, Jewsbury assumes a guiding voice. As an author and professional reader, she relies on her ability to read people: "It is my *business* & profession to know people by *indications* of character" (7076, 19 March 1861?, National library of Wales), and by that means she can suit her style to her audience. She is not writing to an equal, but perhaps writing to someone she could think of as a daughter. At the start of their correspondence Jewsbury wants to protect her from a recent event that has caused Johnes pain, most likely a broken engagement. Jewsbury reveals no evidence of the religious skepticism shown in her early letters to Thomas Carlyle; rather, she suggests that Betha rely on faith in God to overcome earthly grievances. Jewsbury recommends the reading of Thomas á Kempis and the passage of time to heal

Johnes's wounds; she does not draw on her own disappointments in life for example, or harp on the problems for women in this world, but looks to the traditional means of overcoming sadness for women.

As she did with Welsh Carlyle and Mantell, Jewsbury sought to encourage Johnes to write. As Johnes was single, writing would give her the ability to make her life "fruitful & contented" and help her to "become the *best* of *what she has it in her* to become": "No one can have talent & be without a definite object on wh to *work* it out without more or less morbid depression – a sense of waste & loss & a dull unexpressed sense of *remorse* at not adequately using those powers – Where we are not wives or mothers we need *work* we women – & work worth doing if it is to satisfy us" (7081, undated, National Library of Wales). Jewsbury was bringing the same lessons she tried to inculcate in her readers to her friend. Women, Jewsbury believed, need to have a sense of their worth within themselves and also in the eyes of the world.

Jewsbury appeals to Johnes's strengths, grooming someone from another generation to express herself and to pass along the legends of the past. She clearly outlines the difficulty of the task of writing, the need for time alone and focus:

> – Now if you wd. please sit down in yr little room / put away letters – … & begin to write an account of Dolaucothi & all the Legends & traditions of the place & neighbourhood the *glen* where we went – & all as far as Cahir. Don't think of how it will read in print – but just write it all out – dash into the midst of things – & call the paper "*A Bit of the Old World*" That one spot of Dolaucthi wd make & most fascinating paper – Just the story of the place beginning with either the Phoenicians? Or the Romans – Why the air is *thick* with Legends. (7093, 12 February 1869, National Library of Wales)

Having been impressed with the stories Johnes told her when on the estate, Jewsbury anticipates results that she could send to a publisher. But what she receives from Johnes is not as expected and Jewsbury attempts to explain how to improve her writing by first praising what is good about it and then suggesting she change what does not work. Her writing lacks the immediacy Jewsbury felt when told the tales, "it wants *feet* to *walk with* – in other words my dear it wants topographical reality – The descriptions of scenes & places & things are like landscapes in the clouds wh are as beautiful & more suggestive than any landscapes of earth & water – but they fade away & have no substance of solidity." She believes that Johnes has written "not *what you had to say* but what you thought wd be an *appropriate method*" so that the result is neither grounded nor natural (7096, 19 August 1869, National Library of Wales). Jewsbury attempts to be kind and encouraging and tries not to offend Johnes and fears she is not making herself clear. Jewsbury gives advice much as she did to authors when reading manuscripts, in a kindly and also controlling way.

Although she was not successful in her attempts to encourage Welsh Carlyle, Walter Mantell, or Betha Johnes to write, she was successful with the actress Helena Saville Faucit, Lady Martin (1817–98), who published *On Some of Shakespeare's Female Characters* in 1885. As Faucit explains in the introduction, her discussions of the first three Shakespearean characters were written as letters to Jewsbury and arose out of conversations with her as Faucit attempted to put into words the manner in which she had acted the characters on stage:

> Geraldine E. Jewsbury, the valued friend here referred to, had often pressed me to put into writing the substance of what I had said when we talked together of Shakespeare's heroines. She had seen me embody most of them upon the stage, and knowing how much of my inner life had gone into these impersonations, it pleased her to think that I might in

writing do something to awaken in the minds of others the impressions which had grown up in my own through the reverent study of the best part of my life, and been tested and confirmed by the, to me at least, vital experience of the stage ... But my friend, I knew, was dying, and how could I resist her kind assurances that I might do good by yielding to her wish? When I consented, this gave her genuine pleasure; and her pleasure, when she read what I had written, was expressed in words that encouraged me to make it public. (1899: viii)

The result was a popular book that Jewsbury did not live to see published. Jewsbury had been the inspiration for the book, and the relationship and the discussions added to Jewsbury's own pleasure and understanding.

As Jewsbury appears in her letters, she is revealing of her emotions and encouraging to others. With each of her three correspondents discussed here, she appears in a different guise. She courts Welsh Carlyle, remaking herself to avoid the subjects of men and sex that Welsh Carlyle did not want to consider. Eventually they developed a relationship of equality in which Jewsbury could discuss her ideas about women. While writing to Walter Mantell, Jewsbury attempts to appear at times as an Angel in the House, longing for his approval and leadership. Yet when he criticizes her or thinks ill of her, she rushes to justify herself and assert her own mind. In both relationships the sense of Victorian gender borders often becomes blurred and they relate to each other, at their best, as human beings. Jewsbury seeks a community of equals, but adapts herself to her correspondent. With Betha Johnes, Jewsbury becomes a mentor to enable her to become a woman of the future, as she did with the readers of fiction, both in her own works and through her reviews and reports on publisher's manuscripts (discussed in the following chapters). Jewsbury encouraged her correspondents to write and to share themselves with future generations as she did. Never bored nor boring, always finding new interests and new friends, Jewsbury uses her letters to cement and enhance her relationships, the cornerstone of her emotional life. More than just recording her own thoughts, movements, social engagements, and relationships, she seeks to increase the circle of friends and degree of intimacy to form a community of interest. In an era in which women were polite and reserved, differential around men, Jewsbury stands apart as a woman seeking to make a path forward.

CHAPTER 5

Jewsbury as a Reviewer and Editor: Forwarding the Cause of Women

> Nobody can be made free by acclamation or Act of Parliament. Both men and women must work out their own freedom, as well as their own salvation; it cannot be done for them ... The thorough education and cultivation which is now called for on behalf of women, as well as for men, is the real need of both.
> —Geraldine Jewsbury, review of *A Brief Essay on the Position of Women*, by Mrs. C. H. Spear (*Athenaeum*, 24 November 1866: 675)

Because of her reliance on the value of the individual rather than a movement of women, Jewsbury is not recognized enough as a Victorian feminist. Jewsbury believed that laws did not need to be changed in order for women to be "made free". Instead, each individual woman must emancipate herself from her own limited education, ideas, and beliefs. In order to facilitate women in this struggle, Jewsbury slanted her writing towards women, encouraged them to live moral lives, and modeled that behaviour herself as a friend and professional woman. While writing letters, fiction, and articles, Jewsbury also published book reviews for the

Athenaeum from the mid-1850s to 1880 and reviewed manuscripts for the publisher Bentley and Son. She forged a unique career that influenced every aspect of publishing. She went from having her name before the public to being an anonymous presence in the industry, but she continued to support and encourage women.

Through her reviews of fictional works, Jewsbury recommended books to readers that she believed would be helpful to their development as moral individuals, and in her reviews of books directly on the subject of women, commonly called the Woman Question, she voiced her opinion on women in general. She described the Woman Question as concerning women's "natural tendencies, possibilities and prospects in this life" (review of '*Woman: What She Has Been*', *Athenaeum*, 2 August 1862: 139). In addition, she brought two prominent but very different women, Lady Morgan and Caroline Herschel, to the attention of the reading public by editing books about them. Jewsbury invented a multifaceted career for herself and became the preeminent nineteenth-century woman of letters, influencing the reading of her own and another generation of women.

Many literary scholars of the 1970s and 80s thought Jewsbury to be "concerned solely with upholding the Victorian's 'prudish standards of morality'" (Roberts, 2005: 410).[1] They found it ironic that the woman who declared "herself born without any sense of decency" came to be an arbiter of reading material for mid-Victorian women. For example, Fryckstedt believes Jewsbury's reviews "mirror the preferences and prejudices of a middlebrow reader endowed with unusual expertise" (1986: 15) for a reading public of "conventional and conservative taste" (1986: 16) as "her moralistic outlook on fiction was identical with the editorial policy of the magazine in the 1850s, her rigid standards may have become an anachronism in the 1860s when the craze for sensation novels threatened to drown the mainstream of domestic fiction" (1986: 33). Other scholars believe Jewsbury kept a feminist perspective in her reviews (Fryckstedt, 1983; Roberts, 2005; Cary,

1974). Roberts explains: "a closer look at her critiques reveals that Jewsbury was not so much concerned with propriety as with the frivolous portrayal of women's capabilities" (2005: 410). Jewsbury wanted heroines presented as "rational human beings" who use their intelligence and morality rather than their "sentiment and sensuality" (Roberts, 2005: 411). Jewsbury favored education and employment opportunities for women, and particularly the development of woman as moral individuals, and wanted heroines to model those roles.

As previously observed, Jewsbury's feminist beliefs aligned with those of Mary Wollstonecraft who had published *A Vindication of the Rights of Woman* in 1792. She was not on the cutting edge of the movement during the later part of the nineteenth century, but she was nonetheless a feminist. With her reviews, her reader's reports, and her editing, Jewsbury supported women by encouraging them to question the dictates of society and to lead ethical lives.

During the 1850s and 60s innumerable writers, many of whom have been forgotten today, produced and published novels and other works. The readers of these books, composed of people with the leisure and time to read, were confronted with an onslaught of titles. Which ones to read? Several literary weeklies, the *Athenaeum*, the *Spectator* and the *Saturday Review* provided reviews, but "[i]n fact, only the *Athenaeum* among the three weeklies could claim to mirror the vast scene of minor fiction" (Fryckstedt, 1986: 23, n. 6). The *Athenaeum*, a weekly periodical from London, was filled with reviews of literary works and articles of cultural interest. "Called by its editors the 'mirror of Victorian culture' and by George Moore 'the first literary journal in the English language' …, the *Athenaeum* was the most respected and influential critical journal of its time" (Casey, 1996: 151–52). For most of the time that Jewsbury wrote for the *Athenaeum*, William Hepworth Dixon was editor of the journal and they had a personal as well as a professional relationship. She felt he supported her work. Jewsbury wrote to Walter Mantell, suggesting that others on the staff were more likely to shorten her reviews: "[t]he athenaeum is just come I think Mr. Dixon must be home again for they have printed my things this week with some shew of respect and have not snipped off anything" (Dunn, vol. 7, 15 September 1858[?]). Jewsbury probably had been introduced to the editors of the *Athenaeum* by her friend Lady Morgan who had written reviews for them. Jewsbury had another connection on the staff as well: the music critic, Henry Fothergill Chorley, had been introduced to an earlier editor of the *Athenaeum* by Jewsbury's sister, Maria Jane, who had also written for the periodical, and Chorley may have returned the favour to her sister.

Jewsbury became the most important female critic for the journal, and "few reviewers, and no other woman reviewer" during the mid-nineteenth century were as prolific as Jewsbury (Fyckstedt, 1986: 15). Between 1849 and 1880 she published approximately 2300 reviews in the *Athenaeum* (Fryckstedt, 1986: 13). Although published anonymously, her contributions have been established through the discovery of a "marked file", a copy of issues of the journal with the names of the authors written in the margins. However, the attributions are not completely reliable as only surnames are given, the handwriting is difficult to read, and the sheets have been cut after the names inscribed so that "Jewsbury" can become "wsbury" and may be another reviewer altogether (Fryckstedt, 1986: 9).[2]

From the mid-1850s Jewsbury wrote the "New Novels" section of the periodical but her reviews also appear under "Literature", "Our Library Table", and "Books for Children". She reviewed books by such popular writers as George Eliot, Anthony Trollope, Wilkie Collins, George Meredith, Mrs. Gaskell, and Margaret Oliphant, as well as other books by and about women, books for children, biographies, travel, cookery, and odds and ends. Nearly a third of Jewsbury's book reviews were of children's books, according to Lewis C. Roberts (2016). Jewsbury enjoyed reading and writing about books for young people, especially towards the end of her reviewing career when adult literature was moving towards the sensation novel which she disliked because of the prominence of the immoral or amoral heroine, and children's literature was changing to become more imaginative. By the 1870s her eyesight weakened and books for children were generally published in larger typeface and shorter length, making them easier for her to read. In her first "Books for Children" column in 1854, Jewsbury declares: "It requires the finest tact and instinct to write well for children, and so far from being a loss of dignity, it is our opinion that they are the only works for which a superior spirit would not disdain to turn author. When children's books are really good, grown people can read them with as much pleasure and profit as children" ("Books for Children", *Athenaeum*, 25 March 1854: 373). Even though children's literature had not yet achieved the creative glory reached by Lewis Carroll in *Alice in Wonderland* (1865),[3] Jewsbury treats children's literature seriously and frequently remarks about guiding children in their reading. Many books for children were reviewed together, especially near Christmas, leading to short reviews that addressed the adults who would buy the books and suggested books to be given as gifts or prizes for performance at schools. As an author of two novels for children or young adults (see chapter 3), Jewsbury thought frequently about the importance of literature for children throughout her career. In 1853 Jewsbury published a novel for young females, *The History of an Adopted Child*, and in 1855 she published her novel for boys, *Angelo, or the Pine Forest in the Alps*. While her novel for boys emphasizes religious morality, her novel for girls presents a similar lesson to her novels for adults, cautioning them of the stumbling blocks ahead.

Jewsbury reviewed books on such traditional female topics as cookery and dress. She acknowledges the usefulness of cookery books as a single or redundant woman who enjoyed entertaining friends, did not employ a chef, and lived on a moderate income. In describing the subject in one review she writes: "Cookery is not merely 'the art of providing dainty bits to fatten out the ribs,' as the scornful old proverb has it: it is the art of turning every morsel to the best use; it is the exercise of skill, thought, ingenuity, to make every morsel of food yield the utmost nourishment and pleasure of which it is capable" (review of *Mrs. Beeton's Book of Household Management*, 19 July 1862: 79). Jewsbury appreciates the work of cookery as much as any other work, and emphasizes that cooking, like writing, should be undertaken with care.

From her extensive writing and reading, Jewsbury knew the way in which novels were put together, the means by which character were revealed, and was familiar with many novels. Her reviews begin with a general statement about the work, which is followed by a discussion of characters and plots, and ends with a remark on the readership for the book. An overall assessment of the work frequently involves a comparison to other works by the same author. She often remarks on the tone or author's style, objecting to works that are boring or depressing. Jewsbury included long extracts from books in her reviews in order to allow the reader to decide on his or her own reaction to the work (Dames, 2009). Jewsbury ends a review of *Heartsease* (1854) by Charlotte Mary Yonge, with a long quotation and the words: "This extract shows the descriptive faculty of the writer, and justifies the judgment we have passed on it" (18 November 1854: 1397). When writing about *Hide and Seek* (1854) by Wilkie Collins, Jewsbury does not provide a quote and concludes: "it is useless to extract passages from a work which every one should read" (24 June 1854: 775). In her reviews, according to Nicholas Dames, Jewsbury looked at believability, rationality, and emotional appeal, not what the author intended but what the reader experienced (2009). Each reader must decide on whether to read the work or not, but Jewsbury always gives her own opinion. She took her duty seriously, recommending most highly those works that are not just entertaining, but set the reader on a moral path.

Jewsbury's review of George Eliot's *Adam Bede* (1859), her most laudatory review of a work of fiction, begins: "The works of true genius seem the most natural things in the world – so right, that one cannot imagine them different ... 'Adam Bede' is a novel of the highest class. Full of quiet power, without exaggeration and without any strain after effect, it produces a deep impression on the reader, which remains long after the book is closed" (26 February 1859: 284). She immediately discusses the influence of the novel on the reader, detailed from her own reaction to the novel, and comments: "The duty of a critic is in the present instance almost superseded by the reader", suggesting how involved she became with the work. She continues by discussing the character of Adam Bede himself, and quoting a long description of him from the novel in order to give the reader the flavour of reading the novel, and takes from the description the importance of such substantial men and women to England itself. Jewsbury then depicts the heroine, Hetty Sorel, who is flawed, but sympathetic to the reader, and writes that "The Author of 'Adam Bede' has the gift of charity in perfection, without any lack of discernment" (26 February 1859: 284). After commenting on the minor characters in the novel, she describes the arrival of Arthur Donithorne with the reprieve, which "gives the reader a shock that is decidedly painful", and which she states is not handled as well as the rest of the work. But her criticism is slight and she concludes by stating: "it is very seldom we are called on to deal with a book in which there is so little to qualify our praise" (26 February 1859: 284). Jewsbury compliments Eliot's portrayal of country life, her sympathy for her characters, the story itself, but objects to the melodramatic elements of the novel. She finds the depressing aspects of the novel, undoubtedly the infanticide (which she does not mention so as not to give away too much of the plot) and the reprieve from execution, too "melo-dramatic and traditional". Jewsbury believes the brutal facts of the story should be "softened to fit them for their place in a work of Art" (26 February 1859: 284). The modern reader might find the infanticide softened enough as it is, and agree that the last minute nature of the reprieve is too melodramatic. Jewsbury's review does well in capturing the heart and readability of the novel, as well as its sympathetic and moral overtone, all of which she trusted would be of benefit to a reader.

Jewsbury acknowledges the majesty of the works of George Eliot, beginning with her review of *Adam Bede*. Each subsequent novel of Eliot's that Jewsbury reviews is compared to *Adam Bede* and found excellent on its own, but wanting in comparison. Reviewing *Romola* (1863), Jewsbury feared that although the novel would be improving for its readers, it might be too intellectual for the average reader and consequently not "entertaining": "There are noble things to be found in 'Romola,' which will make the reader's heart burn within him. It will be scarcely possible to rise from the perusal without being penetrated by the 'joy of elevated thoughts,' without feeling a desire to cease from a life of self-pleasing, and to embody in action that sense of obligation, of obedience to duty, which is, indeed, the crowning distinction that has been bestowed on man, the high gift in which all others culminate" (1 July 1863: 46). The elevation of moral thought produced by *Romola* embodies Jewsbury's ideal for novels as it encourages moral behaviour in the reader, but she acknowledges that the majority of readers may not be sophisticated enough to enjoy such a difficult work.

Always in her reviews, as in her other works, Jewsbury encourages the best in people. Thus she dislikes Thackeray's *Lovel the Widower* (1860, reviewed by Jewsbury 7 December 1861) because it shows the worst in people without helping readers to become better. She finds this particularly egregious as Thackeray, a talented and established writer, should use his literary power for better purpose. Although she enjoys Anthony Trollope's *The Warden* (1855), she objects that he does not ultimately clarify how he would have his readers think about the different moral positions expressed in the novel: "it is the grave fault in this lively, pleasantly written book, that the right and wrong of the subject are melted down into a matter of perfect indifference" (27 January 1855: 107). The reader should be able to take away a moral from the novel.

In her review of *The Story of Elizabeth* (1863) Jewsbury finds the idea of a mother and daughter falling for the same man to be something that borders on incest and which "is, or ought to be, quite inadmissible for a novel". She recognizes the cleverness of the story but "had it been less clever and more genial, there would have been the germ of greater promise; as it is, it remains to be seen whether the cleverness and facility of style will mature into a deeper and gentler habit of thought and expression" (25 April 1863: 552). Jewsbury did not like a subject she found distasteful to appear in a novel unless it was used to make a moral point that would be improving to the reader. The anonymity of the reviews gave protection to the reviewers, but also gave readers the sense that a review was more than one's person opinion. *The Story of Elizabeth* was published anonymously, but the author of this novel was Anne Thackeray (later Ritchie), the daughter of William Makepeace Thackeray. The negative review upset W. M. Thackeray, and he suspected the reviewer was the writer John Cordy Jeaffreson. In his memoirs, Jeaffreson states that following the publication of the review, Thackeray treated him coldly. Jeaffreson could not tell Thackeray the identity of the reviewer as the writers "were in those days under an obligation of honour to refrain from avowing their contributions to the journal, and also to refrain from saying anything that might be likely to sacrifice in any respect the anonymity of the paper's judgments" (1893: vol. 1, 310). The review became part of a Victorian hostility known as the "Garrick Club Affair" which stemmed from the rivalry between Charles Dickens and W. M. Thackeray. But Jeaffreson blames the review for something more serious: it "may perhaps be regarded as one of the several indirect causes of Thackeray's death before the end of the year" (1893: vol. 1, 309). Although this is an unusual case, the fallout from Jewsbury's review shows the importance a review can attain – a power that she sought to use for the advancement of individuals.

Within each review Jewsbury seeks something positive to point out, and Jewsbury knew readers sometimes sought lighter fare. Quoting a passage from Trollope's *The Bertrams* (1859) "as a specimen of the style", she recommends the novel more for the style than the plot, which "is merely the support over which the vine is trained" (26 March 1859: 420). On George Meredith's *The Ordeal of Richard Feverel* (1859) she admits she did not enjoy reading it, but was compelled to do so, that it is very clever, and "we hope the author will use his great ability to produce something pleasanter next time" (9 July 1859: 48). In Jewsbury's view, novels must both be entertaining and morally uplifting. She describes novels as "amusing" and "readable" and suggests that a lighter novel would be appropriate for reading at the beach. Jewsbury frequently mentions in her reviews whether subscribers to Mudie's, the circulating library of the time that specialized in three-volume moral tales, would be interested in a novel. As in her review of *Romola*, Jewsbury recognizes that many readers might not be as sophisticated or well-educated as she, and consequently praises novels suitable for family fare.

For Jewsbury, every part of a work was connected with its moral. She describes the connection between tone and moral in Elizabeth Gaskell's *A Dark Night's Work* (1863): "Now, a book that depresses spirits instead of bracing the energies and inspiring the reader with a brave cheerfulness, cannot be said to have a successful moral" (30 May 1863: 708). Jewsbury wants characters to distinguish between right and wrong and to be rewarded or punished for their behaviour. She sought to encourage her female readers to better themselves and lauded novels that would forward this purpose through their depiction of character and morality.

Jewsbury negatively reviewed novels by Ouida (the pseudonym of Maria Louise Ramé) and Mary Elizabeth Braddon that became popular with readers. She recognizes their appeal to the reader, but believes they do not measure up to the best literature. Following a retelling of some of the plot of *Under Two Flags* (1867), Jewsbury ends the review: "Ouida has certainly the gift of speech; and though her speech is not standard silver, it is capital electro-plate, and her nonsense has a spirit and dash about it which keep the reader from finding flaws or asking questions" (15 February 1868: 249). Although she recognizes the readability of this novel and the author's talent in creating "spirit and dash", Jewsbury cannot recommend the novel to readers, because of the unrealistic characters, the jargon, and the hectic and repetitive nature of the action. This novel is still enjoyable today, but lacks the high literary merit of an *Adam Bede*. Jewsbury writes of Braddon's *Charlotte's Inheritance* (1868) that it separates into two stories, the first being pleasant and romantic, the second, "an extremely disagreeable story, and it has nothing to redeem its coarse reality; it is left naked, bare and ugly, without even the mellowing touch of time to disguise its harsh and sordid hideousness" (21 March 1868: 418). In part this is a reaction of squeamishness stemming from Jewsbury's dislike of the ugly and depressing, here shoddy investment schemes and poisonings. Although the good prosper and bad repent or die, the whole is unsatisfying because the reader never believes in the characters. Jewsbury recognized the power of Braddon's writing, but this work she finds less involving than other novels by Braddon.

Jewsbury often focused on the nature of the heroine in her reviews. In her review of the anonymously published *Out of the Depths: the Story of a Woman's Life* (1859), Jewsbury describes the heroine as one of the "'unfortunate females' instead of those maiden fortresses of female virtue" (20 August 1859: 240). Although Jewsbury mocks the notion of perfect heroines by talking of the "maiden fortresses of female virtue", she does not approve of the bid for empathy for the "unfortunates" or fallen women in fiction for family fare. Her objection is not to the depiction of prostitution *per se*, but for the moral developed from it. She believes this novel shows no real insight into the "social evil" nor any solution for the problem and thus uses the unfortunate for sensation value only. In her review of *Adam Bede* (*Athenaeum*, 26 February 1859), Jewsbury mentions the sympathy with which the heroine, Hetty Sorrel is drawn, but fails to mention that she is a fallen woman. The morality of the novel is not in question for two reasons: there is another heroine, Dinah Morris, who ends up with the hero and Hetty suffers for the consequences of her fall. Hetty is neither a prostitute nor is she rewarded in any way for her sin. Although her soul is saved, she is punished and changed by the experience. Earlier in the century, fallen women, such as the heroine of Elizabeth Gaskell's *Ruth* (1853), suffered for their transgressions and never found the happiness of marriage, but by the 1860s, this had started to change.

Although many of the novels of the time were published anonymously or with a "by the author of …" statement, the majority of novels reviewed in the *Athenaeum* by Jewsbury were by women (Roberts, 2005: 399), and she lashes out against female writers who do not provide a heroine worthy of emulation or a clear moral for female readers. Jewsbury begins her review of *Woman against Woman* (1865) by Florence Marryat: "It is curious that the most questionable novels of the day should be written by women. To judge from their books, the ideas of women on points of morals and ethics seem in a state of transition, and consequently, of confusion" (17 February 1866: 233) She recognizes a change in the nature of the fiction being published and does not approve of it. Summing up *Woman against Woman* Jewsbury writes: "There is a good deal of ingenuity shown in the incidents of the story, and the tale is written with ease and spirit; but all principle of duty and perception of the difference between right and wrong are wanting throughout the book" (17 February 1866: 233). Better, Jewsbury believes, to present a heroine who could serve as a model for future tempted women to discourage them from becoming fallen. Reading *Woman against Woman* today, the plot seems ingenious, but too much so because the author withholds information from the reader that would explain the seeming misbehaviour of the characters. As Jewsbury suggests in her review, the answer to the puzzle is obvious to the reader before it is revealed at the end when confessions make all clear. The heroine is not fallen, but allowed to appear so for most of the novel. The only fallen woman is from the lower class; she has had a child out of wedlock. Although the proceedings of the novel may appear to be "questionable", this for Jewsbury is because the heroine does not act like a rational woman, but allows the conflicts to happen without being honest. Jewsbury may, in part, have disparaged this novel because of her dislike of Marryat's earlier novel, *Love's Conflict* (1865), that she read for the publisher Bentley and Son as discussed in the next chapter.

Along with morally-dubious heroines, graphic depictions of passion became more frequent in novels later in the nineteenth century. The wave of sensational novels in the 1860s presented heroines who do not do their duty and suffer in silence while acknowledging their errors. The action in sensation novels partakes of the melodramatic, replete with adultery, bigamy, insanity, and murder, but these events occur within the realistic framework of the domestic sphere. Often the docile-looking heroine is the perpetrator of the misdeeds. With sensation fiction the problem of the bored, unhappy heroine is often solved by her running off with a man, whereas Jewsbury wanted the heroine to come to an understanding of herself and her situation. Jewsbury's review of Rhoda Broughton's *Cometh up a Flower* (1867) displays another of her common complaints about the heroines of many sensation novels. Objecting to the literary exhibition of women's sexuality, Jewsbury incorrectly assumes the author: "is not a woman, but a man, who … shows himself … ignorant of all that women either are or ought to be". She sees the novel's "sensual sentimentality" and "self-indulgent emotion" as stereotypical of a masculine view of women's lives: "The only two phases of existence which the author, in his assumed feminine character, seems to think women recognize are, the delight of being kissed by a man they like, and the misery of being kissed by one they don't like. These two points seem to fill up his idea of the whole duty of women" (20 April 1867: 514–15). Jewsbury believed women should have interests and a duty beyond love. In her own fiction Jewsbury is concerned with women being induced to marry men they do not love, but ignores that aspect of Broughton's work. In this instance Jewsbury does not view the totality of the work because of her dislike for the presentation of the heroine. In many of the books of the day, according to Jewsbury, the heroines cannot be a part of a tradition of women helping other women. Jewsbury uses her reviews to encourage writers to set a positive example for their readers and encourages readers to seek out those novels which will enable them to better themselves.

While reviewing Sarah Stickney Ellis's work of fiction embodying ideal women, *Chapters on Wives* (1860), Jewsbury gets at the heart of the problem of wives who can never relax or be themselves, but always act as if they were inferior to their husbands: "Womanhood can never develop into its full nature and capacity under such a system of domestic administration, nor can a man become anything but a well-managed tyrant: his selfishness developed and exploited, – his faults adroitly given way to, – the woman afraid to utter her own thoughts, – no real companionship, – no outspoken friendship as between two rational beings, but a constant ducking to avoid collision, – the truth never quite told, – always a veil, a reticence, a something that is like reality, but not the reality itself" (14 July 1860: 53). She had written to Welsh Carlyle on 22 November 1849: "some day I hope to be able to have a 'say' at Mrs. Ellis and all her school, and develop my own theory more at length. We only want to be let alone, and then we shall neither be 'strong-minded' women nor yet dolls" ([22 November 1849], Ireland, 1892: 320). Jewsbury saw that Mrs. Ellis's type of woman was artificial, never herself, and always a woman relative to a man, while Jewsbury believed women should be viable on their own and not be expected to marry or to manage or care for a man. Neither "strong-minded" nor "dolls", most women needed education and opportunity and self-motivation with which they could develop on their own to become anything. The right end would come, but perhaps slowly. And as women changed, men would also change.

Jewsbury frequently uses her reviews of non-fiction books as a forum for her own mature ideas about women that were in alignment with those of the *Athenaeum*: "The *Athenaeum* has always done justice to the right of women to become all that heaven has made them capable of being and doing, which is the noblest freedom any human being can possess" (review of *Hertha*, 14 June 1856: 739). The Woman Question was endlessly debated, as Jewsbury states in her review of *Woman: What She Has Been, What She Is, What She Will Be, or What She Ought to Be* (n.d.): "every schoolboy seems to think he can solve all the difficulties of the Woman-question" (2 August 1862: 139). Jewsbury agrees with the author's view of women as the nurturing factor behind the success of men in the past, but she continues: "The misfortune of women in the present day is that of late they are expected to be both men and women at once. In the most earnest and distracting terms they are exhorted to make themselves cooks, artists, architects, doctors of every degree, carpenters, painters, glaziers, apothecaries, chemists, printers – every conceivable variety of human speciality: they are enjoined to be fascinating, to be graceful, to be feminine, to be self-asserting, self-denying, obedient, independent, emancipated – correct in all their accounts, moral, and arithmetical – everything at once". Jewsbury ends her review by asking: "What is the emancipation of women? – what is it proposed to emancipate them from? Will any lady or gentleman tell us?" (2 August 1862: 139). Jewsbury believed that women are free and need to be educated and informed to arrange their own lives, but cannot change overnight to be "everything at once". Women will not be aided by changes in laws or regulations or society as much as by themselves. Yet her words against emancipation were not always so strong, Jewsbury's views waivered to some extent.

She wrote to her friend Walter Mantell advising him to read one of her reviews: "it is worth writing in the A[thenaeum] to have an occasional power of protesting" (Dunn, vol. 7, 15 September 1858). In her review *Of Woman, Her Mission and Her Life* (1852) Jewsbury sounds tired of the talk about what women are and what women want and requests that women be treated as rational, living creatures, as Wollstonecraft had advocated. She observes that although women are "small and easily comprehended entities, quite within the powers of masculine legislation both for their souls and bodies, – though, to be sure, Nature has, by way of compensation, given them the faculty of never minding what is said to them!" (18 September 1858: 360). Although legally within the legislation of man, Jewsbury believes women do not need to obey them. Women are free to do with themselves as they like.

In a review contrasting two feminist works, *A Letter to the Queen on Lord Chancellor Cranworth's Bill* (1855) by the Hon. Mrs. Norton and *Women in the Nineteenth Century; and Kindred Papers Relating to the Sphere, Condition, and Duties of Woman* (1845) by Margaret Fuller Ossoli, Jewsbury finds the works opposite in tone and spirit. While the American, Fuller Ossoli, appeals to women to help themselves and each other to seek the highest in marriage, Norton appeals to "noble-hearted Englishmen" for the right to divorce, using her own experience as a lever for change. Jewsbury agrees with Norton that the laws relating to the personal property of women should be changed and notes Norton's dismay that her husband can claim the copyright to the work under discussion (14 July 1855: 811–12). Although Jewsbury did sign a petition in favour of the Married Women's Property Act in 1856, as noted in the introduction, Jewsbury relied on change through the individual rather than as a movement.

Jewsbury expresses her unrealistically optimistic view of the world in her review of Mrs. Horace Roscoe St. John in

Englishwomen and the Age (1860): "If a nation, a class, or individuals be continuously and unrelentingly oppressed – ill used – defrauded of their due share of human benevolence and worldly comfort, there always exists some cause for it – often quite patent, and easy to be discerned. Neither nations nor individuals can be unfortunate long, unless there be some defect in themselves which invites and entertains misfortune" (25 August 1860: 249). Although Jewsbury's ideas here are in accord with many aired early in the nineteenth century, they seem naïve in terms of oppressions such as slavery, an evil with which the oppression of women was compared by both Mary Wollstonecraft (1792) and John Stuart Mill (1869). Jewsbury acknowledges that the author believes, as does she, that women should expand and cultivate their intelligence, but Jewsbury believes that there are no external restrictions and their limitations lie within themselves. Jewsbury agrees with Mrs. St. John that "emancipated" or "self-sustained" women are "disagreeable" as they lack good sense; they do not lack freedom but the judgment to use the freedom they have. Jewsbury believes that the key to "enfranchisement" is the "right to labour on their own account as human beings …" and continues: "It will be a great social revolution when women accept the fact, that when they earn their own living they rise … 'from virtual pauperism to actual participation in the substantial benefits of society'" (25 August 1860: 249). Society itself would change through changes in individual women.

Jewsbury complains in a review of Elizabeth Strutt's *The Feminine Soul: its Nature and Attributes* (1857) that men do not understand women (and neither do many women) as "Men in general, and bachelors in particular, ought to be told that a woman requires a higher motive to lead her life by than even the desire to love, obey, and cook for her lord, – all of which Mrs. Strutt proposes as the chief end of woman" (14 March 1857: 341). Jewsbury dismisses marriage as the center of women's lives. Her argument is similar to that for her dislike of the sensational novel where everything is risked for passion: in both cases women become dependent on men. Jewsbury knew that women could unite to help each other, and illustrates how in all of her work.

Women must start, according to Jewsbury, by obtaining an appropriate education. In her review of Emily Shirreff's *Intellectual Education* (1858), Jewsbury quotes Shirreff's "one suggestion, which marks significantly enough the change that has gradually been taking place in the prospects and condition of the women in this country. She suggests that girls should be educated, not as though marriage were 'their being's end and aim,' but as though marriage were to be the exception, and a single life the rule" (5 June 1858: 714). Jewsbury opposed the traditional attitude that women only need be educated for marriage: "The higher education of women will make a greater change in the habits of society than foreseen. If women are resolved to go in for thorough education like men, they must give up the triumphs of vanity... Love, marriage, and even flirtations, must be postponed: hard work and hard study must be the first consideration. Whether women will be sufficiently 'strong-minded' to incur this cost remains to be seen" (review of *Studious Women* by Monseigneur Dupanloup, 26 December 1868: 882). She worries that not all women have the capacity or fortitude for a career or the ability to give up their lives to a profession. In her review of a *Brief Essay on the Position of Women* (1866) by Mrs. C. H. Spear, Jewsbury seems frustrated by the topic saying that all will fall into place if "the need of education, the thirst for self-improvement, should be awakened within them" (24 November 1866: 674–75). More important to Jewsbury than the specific education itself, was her desire for women to be exposed to higher education rather than to a specific line of study as she believed true for men as well, as expressed in her essay "The Lower Orders" (1847c).

The author of *My Life, and What Shall I Do with IT?* (1860), given on the book only as "an Old Maid" but now known to be Lucy Phillipps, speaks to women who have money and leisure and are bored, and calls upon them to volunteer their skills to help others. Jewsbury begins the review by stating that she has seen so many books on the rights and wrongs of women that "it is a great relief to find that a class of women yet survives who have their material comforts secure, and who have no need to labour for daily bread" (24 November 1860: 702). Jewsbury remarks sarcastically that she has forgotten about those women who do not need to work as of course she, and women like her, struggled to support themselves throughout their lives. This sentiment against upper-class, married women is also expressed in her review of *Woman's Work and Woman's Culture: a Series of Essays* edited by Josephine Butler (1869), in which Jewsbury claims married women have been "the worst hindrances ... to the education and improvement of the condition of women before the law; and it enables men to say that it is only a discontented few who desire to change old laws and customs enacted by men who being father and husband and brothers themselves, must therefore have known what was the best and most desirable things for all" (31 July 1869: 135). Many single women were insecure about their position, desiring to get married, while married women often felt superior to single women and wanted to maintain their feeling of supremacy, thus perpetuating the status quo.

Jewsbury worried about the two and a half million single or redundant women who earned their own livings and needed real jobs. W. R. Greg had written *Why Are Women Redundant?* in 1869, speaking with horror of the redundant woman "who, not having the natural duties and labours of wives and mothers, have to carve out artificial and painfully-sought occupations for themselves; who, in place of completing, sweetening, and embellishing the existence of others, are compelled to lead an independent and incomplete existence of their own" and advocating their emigration to other continents where they would have a better chance of marriage (1869: 5). Jewsbury fought against this belittling attitude, and rather than marriage, advocated for proper education and training for these women. Believing it incumbent upon women without "domestic duties or family responsibilities" to "follow some regular employment," Jewsbury saw that "[w]hen unemployed women take seriously to work, it will bring about a social and political change" (review of *Woman's Right to Labour*, 14 April 1860: 504). She was not, however, ready to rally for enfranchisement; "female suffrage and the franchise for women is that aspect of the question about which we feel least anxiety. Given the education, the disposition to take interest in political and social questions, the franchise will come at the right time, and as a matter of course" (review of *Woman's Work and Woman's Culture*, 31 July 1869: 136). Although she concurred with women seeking change, she believed attention should be paid to the proper education and employment of women.

Jewsbury's own capacity for work was astounding. According to Monica Fryckstedt:

> What puzzles a modern reader struggling through her innumerable reviews, ranking from uninteresting and careless to highly perceptive ones, is the number of books covered. How could anyone, for instance, review eleven novels in one week – January 30, 1858 – four novels and one book on women the following week and eight novels on February 13, 1858? That this could only have been managed by skipping and skimming is quite clear. Nonetheless, Miss Jewsbury reveals to Bentley that she was able to read the manuscript of a three-volume novel at one sitting carefully enough to show a knowledge of the entire plot. This explains how she found time at the height of her career to report on some fifty or sixty manuscript novels a year to Bentley, in addition to reviewing over a hundred books for the *Athenaeum*. (1986: 30)

Jewsbury maintained the life style she wanted, remaining part of the literary world and influencing women of her own and the next generation through her reviews of books.

Jewsbury retells lives and stories, making her reviews interesting and easy to read as she extracts not only the essence of the work but provides details that draw in the reader. From her experience not only as a writer, but also as an editor and translator, she understood the effort necessary to produce a work of non-fiction. Near the start of an article on M. Alfred Bonnear's *The Life of Madame de Beauharnais de Miramion* (1870), she isolates the more subtle factors that go into the work: "We will endeavour to give the reader some idea of this remarkable woman, but before doing so, we owe it to the author, the translator, and the editor to thank them for the great care with which they have given brief but sufficient notes upon all the remarkable persons whose names appear in the narrative. Too much credit cannot be given for the care and pains with which this has been done" (6 August 1870: 170). Reviewing *Diaries of a Lady of Quality, from 1797 to 1844* (1864), Jewsbury praises the editor, A. Hayward, who "has done his task with great judgment; there are no anecdotes that can give pain, nor any tales of scandal; he has retained nothing which one could wish forgotten" (21 May 1864: 706). Jewsbury's taste in biography stems from a different era than our own in that she appreciates a blind eye to indiscretions. She had some difficulty in choosing material for the memoir of Lady Morgan (Sydney Owenson), writing to her fellow editor, William Hepworth Dixon: "L.M – was a very lively bird – there are letters wh give to think! ... Why will lovely women stoop to folly & keep their love letters ?????" (William Hepworth Dixon Papers, 1 October 1861, UCLA). Jewsbury refers to Oliver Goldsmith's poem, "When Lovely Woman Stoops to Folly" (1766), which ironically suggests that all a betrayed woman can do is die. Although Jewsbury would not advise suicide after folly, she definitely feels that the burning of one's letters would be prudent.

By working on the biographies of prominent women from earlier eras, Jewsbury hoped to spur younger women to examine their lives. Lady Morgan (1781?-1859) was over seventy when she and Jewsbury met in 1853. According to Jewsbury's biographer, Lady Morgan was "A vain, clattering, frivolous person who lived on social excitement and adulation, she had nevertheless done her share of work too. She once boasted that she had written forty books (many of them were Irish novels), and her energy and kindliness on behalf of others were prodigious" (Howe, 1935: 137). Jewsbury enjoyed her relationship with Lady Morgan, and through the excitement of her social life she met several women who became her own friends and she enjoyed visiting their estates. Jewsbury, an excellent worker herself, also admired Lady Morgan's capacity for work and together they organize her papers in preparation for publication. In the preface to her first work of autobiography, *Passages from My Autobiography* (1858), Lady Morgan states: "I cannot conclude this little appeal to the indulgence of my dear public without acknowledging the services I have derived from the younger energies and clairvoyance of Miss Geraldine Jewsbury, already known to the public by her own charming works" (Howe, 1935: 139). She paid Jewsbury L90 pounds for this work and when she died she left a legacy to Jewsbury of L200 as well as a plot near her own in Brompton Cemetery where Jewsbury was buried. Jewsbury appreciated the inheritance because it showed the fellow feeling that Lady Morgan had for someone who earned her living by literature.

After the publication of *Passages*, Lady Morgan asked Jewsbury to help her prepare her memoirs for publication, but Lady Morgan died before they had finished. The two volumes of Lady Morgan's memoirs, *Autobiography, Diaries, and Correspondence*, were published by Wm. H. Allen in 1862, edited by William Hepworth Dixon and Jewsbury. Much material needed to be organized, as Jewsbury wrote: "How that dear Lady Morgan lived to the end of her life I cannot imagine, for she wrote Diaries enough to have struck Rhadamanthus dumb. He would never have given judgment in her case if he had had to read them" (Howe, 1935: 140). In a letter to Dixon, Jewsbury refers to her own work on the volume as having "headed [the letters] with a mild word of encouragement to the reader" (21 April 1862, Beinecke Library). She found the work tiring, writing to Dixon that she has done the best she can and worries she will be going into a "convent or lunatic asylum" to recover her wits (25 February 1856, UCLA).

In his preface to the memoir, Dixon explained that Lady Morgan had suggested that her friend, Jewsbury, work on her memoirs and he concurred completely with that choice. Jewsbury appended a sympathetic character sketch to the work. When reviews were negative, Jewsbury wrote to a friend, stating her disappointment in the reception of the work: "As to the Memoirs, I am in a state of disgust at the world. Whilst poor Lady Morgan was alive everybody bowed down to her and now she is dead everybody abuses her, and the book is entertaining and people are so busy abusing her that they overlook that fact" (Howe, 1935: 141). Jewsbury felt badly not so much because of her investment in the work, but in the insult to Lady Morgan.

Jewsbury's last substantial work, seen through the press while at Sevenoaks, Kent, and dying from cancer, was Mrs. John Herschel's *Memoir and Correspondence of Caroline Herschel*, published by John Murray in 1876. Mrs. Herschel sent Jewsbury the manuscript in August 1875 asking for her critical judgment and Jewsbury replied that Mrs. Herschel had "been too timid" (Howe, 1935: 192) in the material she had included so that the portrait was too laudatory and without any controversial material. Jewsbury did not have control over the contents as Mrs. Herschel sailed to India to join her husband, leaving Jewsbury to see the work through the press. Jewsbury rearranged Mrs. Herschel's preface and placed it at the end of the work: "keeping as a preface only the part that dealt with the materials for the book and the mode of arranging them" (Howe, 1935: 194). According to Jewsbury's biographer, Jewsbury had written an introduction of her own "which Murray approved, but he thought it should be signed by her initials and not by Mrs. Herschel's. Jewsbury, however, believed that Mrs.

Herschel would not object to have the new preface attributed to her, and so Murray agreed, since she was willing to take the responsibility" (Howe, 1935: 194). Jewsbury, from her work on reviews and manuscripts, was used to working anonymously – she liked to get the job done whether she was recognized for it or not. But Mrs. Herschel did object to what Jewbury had done; Mrs. Herschel disliked that the tone and style of the preface were so different from her own (Howe, 1935: 195). Jewsbury probably thought she was being generous in giving someone else the credit for her work, but in the end it led to confusion and hard feelings, something she always tried to avoid.

In her Introduction, Jewsbury talks about Caroline Herschel's situation as a woman who spent her life supporting her brother, the famous astronomer, William Herschel:

> These helpers and sustainers, men or women, have all the same quality in common – absolute devotion and unwavering faith in the individual or in the cause. Seeking nothing for themselves, thinking nothing of themselves, they have all an intense power of sympathy, a noble love of giving themselves for the service of others which enables them to transfuse the force of their own personality into the object to which they dedicate their powers. (1876: "Introduction")

Jewsbury herself was in many ways a sustainer of others. She used her intellectual and emotional gifts to illuminate a path for other women to follow both in her life and her work. She was devoted to her many friends and to women of the future. In reviewing books she often described the path that she saw open to women as writers and individuals and urged them to follow it while writing negatively of books that emphasized the darker aspects of life. By editing the memoirs of Lady Morgan and Caroline Herschel she brought before the public two very different women, whose lives had taken very different forms. One, born poor and small, had published novels, married, become a member of the aristocracy and still continued to produce books; the other dedicated herself to working in aid of her brother but made significant advances in astronomy herself in the process.

As in all of her work, Jewsbury presents her ideas clearly and forcefully in order to shape the attitudes of a younger generation. Because of not advocating outright emancipation of women, but individual reform, Jewsbury's contributions as a feminist have not always been recognized. At times she was inconsistent in her statements, but as Monica Fryckstedt sums up, "these occasional inconsistencies and inner doubts can hardly detract from our overall picture of Geraldine Jewsbury as one of the most outspoken and progressive fighters for women's rights during Victorian times, and it is only now, one hundred year later, that we can fully appreciate what must have been a hard and lonely struggle" (1983: 59). Jewsbury's work has been slighted and not viewed in its entirety. Her reviews for the *Athenaeum* clarify her opinion on the Victorian debates over the Woman Question, her belief in the need for changes and for women to help women "to become all that heaven has made them capable of being and doing" (Review of *Hertha* by Fredrika Bremer, *Athenaeum*, 14 June 1856: 739). All that women could be and do was restricted not because they were more limited than men, but because each woman, like each man, had her own shortcomings.

CHAPTER 6

Jewsbury as a Publisher's Reader: Reading for Women

> "I can only say that the sooner there is a Day of Public Humiliation ordained – the better!", neither men nor women have a notion of Duty or responsibility, no duty to God or neighbour … the sentiments in the novel are like the nerves of dram drinkers – flaccid until they are strung up by illicit passion or physical sensations … it is an outrage & an insult to art & literature to make them the staple of what ought to be a work of art and literature
> —Geraldine Jewsbury, reader's report on "Such is Life" (BA, Reel 48, 24 June 1871)

At the end of this report for the publisher Bentley and Sons, Jewsbury confesses that she has "written a sermon on the determination of women's novels" and signs off as his "faithful reader" (BA, Reel 48, report on "Such is Life", 24 June 1871). As in all of her work, in accordance with her feminist beliefs, Jewsbury strove to entertain women, educate them, and prepare them for their lives, supporting those at a disadvantage in society. She believed books should show women who lived as her readers did, and model behaviour to help them with their lives. She was delighted to promote books written by women that would be helpful to women; she was outraged by books written by women who had no writing ability, or who used that ability in a way that she disapproved of.

Jewsbury's reports for Bentley are structured like her reviews for the *Athenaeum*; they concern books written for a similar audience and were written during the same time frame. In a few instances, as with Ouida's *Under Two Flags* (1867), she reviewed a book in the *Athenaeum* that she had previously read in manuscript form. She worked with her friend Lady Llanover on her manuscript of *The Autobiography and Correspondence of Mary Granville, Mrs. Delany* (1861), saw it through the press at Bentley, and then applied to the *Athenaeum* to review it, but was refused as she was a friend of the author (Rosenmayer, 1970: 330). The reports are less finished and frequently contain extraneous information, but they focus, like the reviews, on the plot, character, and style of the works under consideration and their possible influence on readers. She seeks to make known to readers the best among the works she considers, in order to amuse and, if possible, to enlighten them.

The majority of Jewsbury's reviews take the form of letters to the Bentleys giving anything from a quick dismissal to a detailed report on the works before her. In her reports Jewsbury combines her professional with her personal thoughts. At times she describes the difficulty of sending manuscripts and reports back and forth across the country as she visited friends. Typically of Jewsbury, her working relationship also became a friendship, and she often begins or ends her letters by inquiring after the health of everyone in the Bentley family. However, she rarely mentions her own activities, other than those like traveling or being sick, that might interfere with her receiving or working on manuscripts.

The exact scope of Jewsbury's job is not known, no written directions appear to have been given, but from the evidence of her reports some ideas can be determined. Jewsbury was a woman working in a man's field and eager to please her employer even though she does at times disagree with him and stands firmly by her opinion. Always, while reviewing, she seeks books that retain traditional values and that maintain the dignity of Bentley and Son, but she looks out for books that are also of a higher literary quality, and that provide a template for how women can deal with the difficulties in their situations. Although, as a publisher's reviewer, she desired to recommend great literature for publication, Jewsbury was limited by the manuscripts she received, the requirements of her job, and the need for publishers to make money.

On 19 October 1858 Jewsbury was in the company of Lady Morgan, working to compile and edit Lady Morgan's *Passages from My Autobiography*[1] when Jewsbury left for an interview with the publishers Richard Bentley and Son. She recounted her day to Walter Mantell: "I went to Lady Morgan she had a grand impromptu soirée last night – & was very gracious but she had gone & lost some MS wh I had laid carefully bye so *I* was *not* gracious. I went & had an interview with the whole house of Bentley. I think they must be pleased with their bargain for they are so civil to me & I don't suppose my own merits have much to do with it" (Dunn, vol. 7, 19 October 1858). Always enjoying an active social life, Jewsbury returned to spend the evening with Lady Morgan in the company of the Duke of Wellington and Charles Villiers.[2] A short time later she began reporting on manuscripts for Bentley and Son, a position she held until she died.

Publisher's readers, also known as "literary advisers", became common during the Victorian era because of the number of unsolicited manuscripts sent to publishers. "The primary function of the publisher's reader was to judge the merits of manuscripts and advising the publisher whether to accept or reject them for publication" (Carney, 1996: 146). As a reader Jewsbury added to the professionalization of publishing by reviewing manuscripts, becoming an intermediary between author and publisher (Roberts, 2005: 413). She dealt primarily with Richard Bentley (1794–1871), the founder of the firm, until he was in a railway accident in 1867. He was succeeded by his son, George Bentley (1828–95), who established a journal, *Temple Bar*, to add to their books. Bentley and Son was the most solid and respectable of publishing houses according to Gordon Ray, however, "several [other publishing houses] appear in retrospect to have achieved more distinguished lists" (1952: 178). Bentley considered their customers as a politer readership than most, and one author, E. G. Curtis, requested that Bentley reissue his works with these words; "I had a pretty fair offer from Messrs Ward and Lock in the City but I should like my books to appear among a higher class of works that those which they publish" (BA, Reel 45, 5 February 1864).

Jewsbury's reviews reveal her concern for the well-being of Bentley and Son, both in terms of its reputation and profits. About a manuscript with no title she writes: "the story is very clumsy & the style is overlaid – the plot is just absurd – the aim is that everybody ought to forgive everybody & everything ... – people wd make great fun of it" (BA, Reel 47, 12 July 1867). Some manuscripts were simply mediocre. "I have of late read several M.S. (wh I will enumerate) any *one* of *wh* you might find it worth while to accept *but* if you were to take them *all*, you wd have a lot of mediocre works on yr hands wh wd lower the value of yr name as a publisher" (BA, Reel 47, 14 May 1863). She is cognizant that she is advising for Bentley's readers, and aware of the monetary considerations involved: "Either a novel had those characteristics which made for broad appeal (and this can be connected with its exploitation of conventions), or it appealed to an interested minority who could be counted on to buy it" (Rosenmayer, 1970: 336). As Linda Marie Fritschner writes, Jewsbury "tried to uphold literary standards within the category of literature as an entertainment or a diversion. Generally, her acceptance or rejection of a manuscript depended upon her evaluation of the commercial potential of the manuscript – the probable reader, the books already on the Bentley list, and the books of other firms"

(1980: 93–94). She writes of one work: "You wd not only lose money but reputation & caste by taking that style of work" (BA, Reel 48, 16 February 1871).

Although she was a trusted advisor, Jewsbury was paid little for her work. According to Fritschner: "Bentley typically paid one guinea for a full report with a suggestion for or against acceptance. This would not have even covered the cost of purchasing a copy of a novel Jewsbury might have recommended, which would have been priced at a guinea and a half" (Roberts, 2005: 414). In order to supplement her payments, very often Jewsbury requests additional books for review or offers to undertake other jobs he may have at hand, such as editing.

No one could be better equipped to be a publisher's reader than Jewsbury. Throughout her life she read widely and quickly, remembered what she read, and could write clearly and decisively. She had herself published six novels, two novels for children, articles for periodicals, book reviews for the *Athenaeum*, and edited several works, and so she knew well how a novel was constructed. She could examine a work to uncover the elements that she believed would make for a good work or one that needed to be revised or rejected. She created 609 written reports from 8 February 1860 to 8 January 1875 covering 809 manuscripts. However, there are clearly missing reports and suggestions in her letters to Bentley that many others were given orally in discussions with the publisher (Fahnestock, 1973: 311).

Jewsbury reviewed mostly novels (predominantly written by women), books of travel, and memoirs. Jewsbury did not make the final determination on the fate of a work; she made a recommendation for publication or not, or explained the factors that Bentley might consider in making a final decision. If Bentley did not agree with her determination or requested more information, Jewsbury sometimes argued her point in a second interaction. She wrote to Bentley: "you know and *I* do *not*, the various reasons wh might induce you to lean on one author, rather than another, or to take a work in one style, in preference to one upon another subject – upon these points you will of course judge for yr self." (BA, Reel 46, 14 May 1863). At times Bentley asked her to read a manuscript in which he had a special interest. She would deliberate carefully and often comment at length, but she would be unsure of the factors he was considering such as friendship with the author or the general interest in the topic. Describing one novel, she states: "reviews will praise it but *nobody* will read it for pleasure or amusement" (BA, Reel 46, 9 March 1861). Or she wonders if a novel would make money and suggests of one of Mrs. Lynn Linton's novels that it is "not pleasant, but it is clever, not a success but a respectable average, let it be a contingency if you accept it" (BA, Reel 47, 18 November 1864). Bentley did not accept the novel, and it was published by Smith, Elder & Co. as *Grasp Your Nettle* (1865). At times Jewsbury requests more information about the author or whether she can receive additional volumes, having been sent an incomplete manuscript.

When reconsidering a manuscript she had read and reported on, Jewsbury's recommendations were usually fixed and her opinion outspoken. A few times she changes her opinion, as when writing about "The Life of Robert Dudley, Earl of Leicester". In her first note she states: "It is taken & transcribed entirely from state papers & old ms. strung together according to date"; the work contains "no narrative so not for the general reader" (BA, Reel 48, 8 March 1872). Four days later she is "rethinking wondering if she said enough in favour of the work ... I myself had been more interested than I was aware of – for I returned to the MS. & read it *all to the end!*" (BA, Reel 48, 12 March 1872). Although impressed by the pains the author took to collect the material, she is still unsure of the readership for the book and wonders if it might not make an article instead. She looked out for shorter works that might be included in *Temple Bar*, published by Bentley, and frequently comments on articles she had read in that journal. Alternatively, she suggests that a novel might make good railway reading like

"Hearts & Homes Changed & Exchanged" (which Bentley never published), "for any pretension to being a work of literature, it has *none*" (BA, Reel 46, 27 June 1862).

Generally, Bentley acted on her advice, however, novels she rejected were sometimes published by other firms. Several, such as the Lady Chatterton's *Retribution* (1861) and Nina Cole's *Which is the Heroine?* (1870), were published by Newby, which Jewsbury considered a lower class of publication; while Tinsley Brothers, a rival to Bentley, published Ouida's *Granville de Vigne* (1863) and Rosa Kettle's *Over the Furze* (1874). After reading her report, Bentley would inform the author of his decision. She often suggests that Bentley might add a note to the author of a work that she dismisses to send the manuscript to Newby.

Jewsbury's overall influence on the novels being read was strongest with those accepted by Mudie's Circulating Library. Bentley and Son made most of their money by selling copies of the three volumes of a novel to Mudie's. Three volumes were the most lucrative format because the volumes would be loaned separately in the hope that the reader would retain interest to finish the work. Jewsbury writes in one letter: "If Fiction were the staple speciality of yr house I shd say take it amongst the rest – but you please remember that this ms contains nothing either powerful or exciting – it will have no run – nor make any sensation nor have any success beyond a mere circulating library existence as a new novel" (BA, Reel 46, 17 June 1863). She distinguishes between those novels which might be briefly popular and those belonging to a higher class of literature.

The readers of the novels were typically women of the middle and upper classes who had the money to purchase books and the leisure to read them. She expects readers to be well-read, for example, she requests Bentley refuse "A Romance of the Court translated from the German", about a "melancholy love affair of the sister of Frederick the great", because she assumes readers would already know the story from reading Thomas Carlyle's *Life of Frederick the Great* (1858) in six volumes (BA, Reel 47, 6 March 1866), a work that few read today. She was unsure of the extent of the readership for some works, wondering if women would be interested in a work on speculation in New York (BA, Reel 46, 9 March 1862). At times she worries that readers would object to the difficult names in works concerning Australia, India, or Ceylon (BA, Reel 46, 26 January 1863; BA, Reel 46, 14 June 1874). She understood that her education and interests might be beyond that of most readers, but assumes that if she enjoys a work, so will the readers.

Jewsbury's reports follow the pattern of giving an overview of the novel and her recommendation and then backing this up by comparison to other works by the same author or other works she had read, discussion of the plot (and especially early on she gives a summary of the plot at length), the style, the readership for the work, the projected profitability of the author, and if her opinion was negative but with some reservations, whether the author might be encouraged to try again. Even in the cases where she was unsure as to whether a book would make money if published, she, as Fritschner phrases it, "assessed, approved, condemned, and dissected manuscripts" with the "attitude of a surgeon. Ruthlessly and incisively she took manuscripts apart" (1980: 59). She laid out her argument to Bentley quickly but carefully.

At times, Jewsbury went beyond her job to bring manuscripts to the attention of Bentley; she suggested to Lady Chatterton and Frances Power Cobbe that they submit manuscripts to Bentley, thereby encouraging the publication of her friends. She explains to George Bentley: "I know that yesterday Friday a M.S. of select readings from Plato was confided to you by Georgianna Lady Chatterton and she sent them to you by *my* advice – I want the public to have the benefit of them especially women to whom so much trash & twaddle is daily administered – What *other* translations I have seen have been heavy & clumsy – *These* are very readable – very intelligible & they *interested me* very much they are really good & *interesting* reading & I really am sorry for the women who have so much rubbish written expressly *a leur intention*" (BA, Reel 45, 17 August 1861). Jewsbury was excited to offer Bentley a prestigious work, one so different from the majority of works that he published for female readers. Chatterton's *Selections from the Works of Plato* was published by Bentley in February 1862. About Frances Power Cobbe, she writes: "She is extremely well known & highly thought of – Trubner has thitherto been her publisher but she is leaving him because she is not pleased with his behaviour to her – & she told me she was looking for another publisher – I advised her to come to you" (BA, Reel 47, 13 March 1868). Bentley decided against publication and Jewsbury responds: "I think there wd have been a *credit* in it if even not great profit – but I stick like a good shoemaker to *my own* Last! & only speak on novels!" (BA, Reel 47, 8 May 1868). This statement suggests that she was hemmed in by the restrictions of her task, that she would have preferred to comment on works that may have included better literature and that were written for a more sophisticated readership than she was selecting novels for. Although she is determined to stand by her job, she speaks out to let her feelings be known. Even if women intend to read "rubbish", they should be encouraged to read a higher class of literature.

Jewsbury approached Margaret Oliphant about publishing in *Temple Bar*: "Today I saw Mrs Oliphant & of my own accord asked her whether she were at liberty now to write a novel for Temple Bar if she were applied to for one. Her answer was quick & frank; – It wd depend on what she was offered but she wd require high terms. I did not enquire what her terms were. I consider that a private matter altogether ... I hope I have not taken a liberty in asking her the question if I did you will have to forgive me" (BA, Reel 46, 12 June 1873). Conscious of other women who, like herself, supported themselves by writing, Jewsbury attempted to help these women. She also approached Bentley on the request of another friend; "By the way, Hepworth Dixon told me I might when I had the opportunity ask you whether you are disposed to entertain a proposal for a work on Japan from him? Of course this is a strictly private enquiry" (BA, Reel 48, 18 May 1873). Through her friendships, Jewsbury influenced the works Bentley published to a limited extent. Always, Bentley had the final say as to publication and payment.

For the most part Jewsbury did not know the name of the author of the manuscripts she read. Only about a hundred reviews mention the author's name (Rosenmayer, 1970: 524). But there were exceptions when Jewsbury knew the author personally. In the case of Florence Marryat, Jewsbury asks that her report be copied over before being sent to the author as she might recognize Jewsbury's handwriting. Once in a while she would encounter an author in the social life of London. She met Mrs. Henry Wood, the author of *East Lynne*, at a party and wrote to Bentley that she was "as *un*like a novel writer as anybody I ever saw!" (BA, Reel 46, 16 May 1862). At another time she saw Annie Thomas, the author of "Sir Victor's Choice", who had sold her book to the Tinsley Brothers: "she is a bright little creature, darting about like a bird, *very* good, supporting her mother & aunt ... *but* she will never do anything of mark – she writes too quickly too much with too little pains – & she has but a very moderate amount of stuff in her" (BA, Reel 46, 13 June 1864). Jewsbury shows sympathy for Thomas's situation, but is critical of her approach to writing; the personal morality of the author was less important than what was conveyed in the work. She had little patience for mediocre work.

Jewsbury sought works that might have a lengthy lifespan but was swamped with works that might be "readable for idle people & even they wd never open the book a second time" (BA, Reel 47, 30 October 1867). Although she recognized better literature, she did not come across examples often. Even for some of the higher-quality manuscripts that crossed her path, she requests small changes to improve the works. Of Emily Eden's journal, which was to become *Up the Country: Letters Written to Her Sister from the Upper Provinces of India* (1867), Jewsbury explains: "It is pleasant & sparkling and very amusing – only there shd be a preface explaining the circumstances of the journey & giving a little sketch of the motives & intentions of the Governor General for taking the journey" and suggests the illustrations the writer mentions be added to show "an India that has passed away" (BA, Reel 47, 16 February 1866).

While working for Bentley, Jewsbury examined works by some of the most famous authors of the era. She recommends Bentley publish two novels by T. A. Trollope (BA, Reel 48, 21 May 1870 and 19 January 1872), although she judges them not as good as his Italian novels. She summarized "Chance or Choice" by Albert Eubule Evans, but warns Bentley: "please *refuse* it unless you wish to furnish critics with a choice morsel to cut into mincemeat & make merry over their task – You see even I, cd not resist telling you some of the story to amuse you only *don't* suppose the book is half as entertaining as my account of it!!" (BA, Reel 48, 1 August 1874). Although Evans published several novels, this one seems never to have made it into print. She recommended Bentley not publish books by several well-known foreign authors: Gustave Flaubert (*Salammbo*, BA, Reel 47, 15 January 1863), Alexandre Dumas, (*Emma Lyons*, BA, Reel 47, 17 November 1863), and Giuseppe Garibaldi, a man she admired, (*Rule of the Monk*, BA, Reel 47, 18 June 1868). She advises against a translation of Alexandre Dumas's *Emma Lyons* (1864), even suggesting Bentley pay Dumas to get out of the bargain as it was weaker than his usual novels and a "coarse common place & highly immoral French novel of the modern type". At first Jewsbury tried crossing out passages, but then found that "all alike was bad except what was worse" (BA, Reel 47, 20 November 1863). These authors were capable of doing much better writing; Jewsbury refused to give them a pass because of their names, but judged the manuscripts before her.

Jewsbury particularly objects to authors she assumes to be young women who have read many novels and so believe they can write one, but have no experience of life and do not approach writing as a serious endeavour. In a world in which Jewsbury wanted male and female writers to be judged by the same yardstick, perhaps she feared they would cast a pall on women writers in general. She complains of "The Days that are Past" that it "is perfect rubbish & it is a species of impertinence in young ladies to trouble publishers with such inane stuff" (BA, Reel 46, 12 April 1862). About "The Lyre & Sword" she comments: "The *idea* is good – & a very good book *might* be made of the subject, ... all the interest has been carefully *omitted* ... *all* the trouble & difficulty has been so carefully *shirked*" (BA, Reel 46, 8 May 1863). Bentley requested more information on "Olive's Love Affair", and Jewsbury responds:

> I can believe she found little difficulty in writing it – the 'easy parts' of a task, of *any* description are those in wh the doer of the task *evades* what wd have made the workmanship better. – If the work be writing a novel, I wd say the *easy* way is to make an epithet or an adjective do the work of an idea, or of an observation properly *thought out* & carefully expressed – all such expressions as "*moaned she*" or "shrieked she" are examples of *idle* work; – patching on incidents by after thought wh ought to have been taken up & inserted at the time, are examples of doing things easily *instead* of thoroughly! ... In writing – an author must endeavour to obtain a distinct idea of what he or she desires to say & to say it distinctly in as few words as possible. (BA, Reel 48, 24 August 1872)

Jewsbury could write freely to Bentley as he did not pass her remarks on to the author without letting Jewsbury know. She believed writing to be a serious occupation which should not be entered lightly as a pastime for moments of idleness; an author should labour and wrestle with the work in order to make the result as good as possible.

Most of the manuscripts were refused and approximately one sixth of the manuscripts Jewsbury refused flatly with little more comment than "Rubbish" (Rosenmayer, 1970: 423). Although she advises not to accept the manuscripts, twenty-six of her reports suggest promise in the writer (Rosenmayer, 1970: 547). When an author had previously published, as with the writer of "Dearly Beloved", she reflects that the novel "is clever but there is a general tone in it wh is not pleasant – like an unfortunate *flavour* in cookery wh mars the taste of good ingredients & spoils the dish… It is just one of those cases in wh the *name* of an author wd turn the scale … the author has of course made her mark on the world – so ask her to write you *something else* but my judgment is against yr accepting *this*" (BA, Reel 46, 27 March 1863). Jewsbury's imagery gives the reader a good sense of the problem with the novel. The easiest rejections were those she had read for another publisher and rejected (Mr. Newman is mentioned twice although the scope of her work for him is not known). Most frequently Jewsbury rejects works because they are uninteresting, boring, pedantic, or depressing. She also objects to a vulgar, flippant style, verbosity, telling too much (as opposed to showing), flat characters or characters that are not lifelike or human, and ridiculous plots.

Jewsbury considered all the elements of a work. If a novel did not meet Jewsbury's approval but had some redeeming element, she often called for revisions, rewrites, and changes. The requested changes concern everything from individual words, grammar, tone, wordiness, descriptions, sentences, paragraphs, titles, to scenes, plots, beginnings, and endings. She would either make the revisions herself or her suggestions would be sent on to the author. Favouring the writing of educated ladies and gentleman, she sought works that would appeal to an educated class as well. Jewsbury's revisions often refer to the coarseness of a character or scene or the vulgarity of words, such as slang or jargon, or sins against good taste.

Often she found the resubmissions were not an improvement. When many of the original problems remained, she asked for even more changes. She called on writers to take more pains with their work, to rethink their novel rather than to make easy corrections. According to Rosenmayer, most of the requested revisions clustered in 1864 and 1865, showing it may have been a policy at the time that did not work out (Rosenmayer, 1970: 461). When she read Florence Marryat's first novel, *Struggle for Life*, Jewsbury filled ten pages with ideas on how to rewrite the novel, and recommends vast plot changes that altered its meaning. She suggests that the novel be retitled, *Enduring to the End*, as she believed characters in novels must recognize and endure the situation in which they find themselves because of mistakes they have made, just as her friend Jane Welsh Carlyle did. Reading the resubmitted manuscript, Jewsbury found it was "weak where it ought to be strong", probably because Marryat did not have her heart in the revisions. Jewsbury particularly objected to the indelicate handling of the pregnant heroine's confinement, and "added to this, there is something disagreeable in the fact brought prominently forward of the heroine receiving ardent declarations of love from the man when she is just going to become the mother of *her husband's child*" and recommends that Bentley refuse it (BA, Reel 47, 2 December 1864). Despite Jewsbury's recommendation that it not be published, the revised novel was published by Bentley as *Love's Conflict* (1865). Catherine Pope has examined the revisions, although the initial manuscript does not exist, and argues that in her later novels and in her role as publisher's reader, Jewsbury's "rhetoric is also disturbingly similar to that employed by politicians who sought to enshrine the sexual double standard in law during parliamentary debates on the legal position of women. Jewsbury has a political, as well as a literary, agenda, acting as a mouthpiece for moral conservatism" (2013: 3). Jewsbury may have been overzealous in her recommendations as the trend in novels changed, but she was always aware that she was recommending novels for a primarily female audience who needed to be encouraged to live moral lives and could be helped in making decisions in their lives by their reading. Her goal was not to keep women enshrined as Angels in the House, but she believed society could be changed through the strengthening of the individual.

Morality was an important component of her considerations, but not the only element she looked at. Writing was important as well. She complains about *Varina*, that the writing "is not good enough to offset bad morality" (BA, Reel 48, 18 February 1861), indicating that she would recommend a book with "bad morality" if the overall writing were better. She writes of William Knox Wigram's *Five Hundred Pounds Reward*: "decided clever & it entertained *me* very well". Although she asks for changes, including the disappearance of a brandy bottle, she concludes: "But you may accept it – for it is a good wholesome story" although "all the moralizing in the first chapter & elsewhere must be curtailed" (BA, Reel 47, 9 April 1867). In her *Athenaeum* review of Trollope's *The Warden* (see chapter 5), Jewsbury declares that the author's point of view was not made clear to the reader. Although the moral stance of the author should be apparent, the reader should not be hit over the head with moralizing. Jewsbury objected to direct moralizing and wanted the reader to take the moral from the events of the novel and the consequences to the characters, although she worked with the material she received.

She describes the end of the novel by the unknown author of "Such Is Life" whom she desired to suffer on the "Day of Public Humiliation": "the heroine accepts the love of a man who certainly is not her husband receives his carresses wh are very ardently described & only does not form the subject of a Divorce scandal because she is drowned whilst on her way to the yacht of her lover and so makes a lovely corpse instead over wh every body sheds tears" (BA, Reel 48, report on "Such is Life", 24 June 1871). The plot is not only unrealistic, but the novel has no message for the reader.

As the century progressed, she found more frequently that the authors did not reward the good and punish the bad and did not take the concept of duty into account. Her response was more complex than might initially appear. Jewsbury, from her early reading of Thomas Carlyle, believed that everyone must do his or her own duty, as described in chapter 1. So that even when she enjoys a novel, and finds *Jack Seavers* "smart & clever", although finding "nothing of *genius* in the story", she does not recommend it be published as, "The *inconvenience* of the permanent marriage tie is the one subject of the story, – not a trace of religion or duty nor of recognition of the *sins* of marrying for money ... it wd *never* help a struggling person but might injure by depressing their faith and in bewildering their principle of right & wrong" (BA, Reel 47, 25 September 1865). For Jewsbury, nothing in the novel mitigates the treatment of the subject.

Jewsbury liked an erring heroine to be redeemed, but such a situation must be adequately prepared within the novel, as in *East Lynne* (discussed presently). This is not the case in *Hearts & Homes Changed & Exchanged*:

> The moral is highly questionable; a woman who has married one man without any affection for the sake of his money, – who abandons him & her child & runs away with another man, with whom she lives till he is tired of her – & then without being divorced marries a second husband whom she drives to dangerous courses; – she endeavours to poison her attendant who knows her secrets – & has a brain fever after which she repents & goes out for a governess – she is a blessing to the family she enters & becomes without any particular reason as estimable as she had been execrable – & she goes back to her husband & is a model Mary Magdalen but without any sort of difficulty – literally no more than "turning over a new leaf". (BA, Reel 46, 27 June 1862)

The heroine of this novel shows no significant remorse for her misdeeds and is never punished for them. Jewsbury found it unrealistic, that a heroine, guilty of adultery, bigamy, and attempted murder, could change simply by "turning over a new leaf". Existing only for the sensational aspect of the plot, the novel has nothing in terms of depth of character to explain the events described.

About *Made in Heaven* (1873), a novel she recommended but Charles Mudie refused to allow in his libraries, Jewsbury explains: "I *know* there were sins against good taste … but so far as the main scope & gist of the work goes, I still keep my opinion that it is *good*". In the novel a woman has been forced by her mother to marry a man she does not love and who is an alcoholic.

> About 'the pathology of delirium tremens' in this book, as it has been called, I really believe if women were able to *realise* all that is meant by a man being 'wild' 'dissipated' 'inclined to drink' & such euphemistic terms, that even Mothers wd shrink from letting their daughters marry such men … so far from being *immoral* I consider these strong unvarnished representations of *what* a husband given to drinking really is – as a *good service* done.

Jewsbury appreciates the honest portrayal of a real difficulty faced by some women and concludes her report: – "The books that *really* ought to be put down are those trashy weak novels in w*h*. there is no real distinction made *palpable*, between right & wrong – & where women shew a constant inability to feel any moral indignation against baseness" (BA, Reel 46, 27 July 1873). Jewsbury believed the novel was rejected by Mudie for depicting a sordid picture of life which readers should not be exposed to, but Jewsbury approved it because its intention was to condemn forced marriages and addictions which are part of life and she had the tenacity to argue her convictions.

Her main objection to "French novels" and sensation novels was that the reader is left with the impression that passion is the most important thing in the world. John Wilson Croker had denounced French novels in an 1836 article in the *Quarterly Review*, stating: "She who *dares to read a single page* of the hundred thousand licentious pages with which the last five years have inundated society is *lost for ever*" (qtd. in Atkinson, 2017: 164). Croker, known for his review of John Keats's *Endymion*, which Percy Bysshe Shelley believed sent Keats to an early grave, certainly overstates the case, but advances a common point of view in England. Thomas Carlyle had expressed a disdain for George Sands's work, indicating that he believed her writing was responsible for Jewsbury's youthful elevation of passion over duty, as described in chapter 1. Jewsbury wished to deny Bentley's readers exposure to this temptation, and to educate them to be better people.

As a reader for the publisher Bentley and Sons, Jewsbury recommended novels to be published that would influence a younger generation of readers. She worried about the effect of books she considered immoral on readers who were less sophisticated and experienced than she. In her youth she had enjoyed the fiction of Sand, but as she aged and felt the responsibility of her position, she feared the effect of "French Novels" on the young, and sensation novels had many of the same troubling features. Although there was little likelihood of young women being spurred to murder by their reading, they may be tempted towards crimes of passion by an author's seeming approval of love outside of marriage and the author's titillating description of sexuality. Consequently, she recommended books that advocated that woman adhere to their duty and that did not deem passion the center of a woman's world.

Bentley had a chance to become the publisher for four of the most popular authors of the late Victorian era, all of whom wrote sensation fiction: Mrs. Henry Wood, Mary Elizabeth Braddon, Rhoda Broughton, and Ouida. They became best-selling authors who made much money for their publishers, and Bentley succeeded in securing two of them. Jewsbury's biggest discovery was Mrs. Wood's

East Lynne, a novel that was a best-seller throughout the Victorian period and beyond. When Jewsbury first read Ellen Wood's *East Lynne* in the *New Monthly Magazine* (published between January 1860 and September 1861), she wrote to Bentley suggesting he publish the work; "I myself have been so much interested as to be anxious to read the conclusion for my own amusement! A testimony to the chance that it may interest other people" (BA, Reel 46, 19 June 1861). However, Jewsbury suggested Bentley require many changes in terms of grammar and "sins against good taste" particularly in regard to Barbara's "violent explosion" after the marriage of the man she loves. Jewsbury thought she should declare herself "in a less violent manner" (BA, Reel 46, 19 June 1861). Jewsbury herself made the corrections, but the novel was published as originally written. She mentions the novel frequently afterwards: "I do not like 'The shadow of ashlydiat' so well as East Lynne – it is better written but the tale is not so fascinating" (BA, Reel 46, 3 January 1862), and she recommended *East Lynne* to her friends as well: "East Lynne is a great favourite in this neighbourhood tho *some* think it very improper & immoral but all agree that it is very amusing & interesting" (BA, Reel 46, 24 April 1862). Although the heroine of *East Lynne* chooses passion over duty and commits adultery, she comes to see the error of her choices, repents, and suffers by losing everything of consequence to her.

To some extent Jewsbury understood the popularity of sensation fiction, and enjoyed it herself, although she worried, a bit hypocritically, that it might be harmful to other women. Jewsbury admired Mary Elizabeth Braddon's *Aurora Floyd* (1863), telling Bentley to buy the manuscript. She found it "superior in point of good writing to East Lynn and quite equal to that novel in strong interest & it will I imagine be quite as successful. You say you want a good novel – here it is for you in Aurora Floyd!" (BA, Reel 46, 14 July 1862) Braddon demanded £600 and Jewsbury recommended not going higher than £300. Jewsbury also enjoyed *Lady Audley's Secret* (1862) although she found it inferior to *Aurora*

Floyd (BA, Reel 46, 29 July 1862). She may have preferred *Aurora Floyd* because of the nature of the heroine: although both Aurora Floyd and Lady Audley commit bigamy, Aurora Floyd acted from youthful indiscretion, mistaken information, and is wrongly accused of murdering her first husband, whereas Lady Audley attempts to kill her first husband as well as a person who has come to learn her secret. Both manuscripts eventually went to Tinsley, who had such high profits from *Aurora Floyd* and *Lady Audley's Secret* that he built himself a villa that he named Audley Lodge (Sutherland, 1989: 80). Jewsbury recommended in favour of the novels, and suggested an amount to offer, but the negotiation was in Bentley's hands and he lost the profits.

Rhoda Broughton's novels lack the extravagant plots of other sensation novels, but focus on youthful passion. She became Jewsbury's particular *bête noir* because her novels were strongly and appealingly written in a manner that Jewsbury thought might be influential to readers. Broughton's uncle was J. Sheridan Le Fanu, one of Bentley's authors and Bentley wanted to oblige him. On receiving *Not Wisely but Too Well* (1867) for a recommendation, she represents the manuscript "as a picture strong of unregulated sensual passion. it is lifelike enough – but the story is absolute and unredeemed nonsense – and the interest is the kind that I shd carefully keep it out of the hands of all the young people of my acquaintance". The tale combines "highly coloured & hot blooded passion" with "a few drops of luke warm rose water sentimentality". She condemns the style of the book:

> it is nothing but a series of love scenes if it can be called & the point of interest turns upon the man being a "big Titan" with "brawny athlete arms" "superb broad shoulders" & "cavernous gleaming eyes" – a thorough black guard contrasting with the heroine who is "little" "round" "soft" with soft white shoulders "soft white arms" "seagreen eyes" a witching form & face – wh the aforesaid "Titan" "crushes"

& "kisses" & "devours" & "holds in iron grasp" & with the little girl herself it is a case of animal magnetism ... It is a *bad style* of book altogether & not fit to be published. (BA, Reel 47, 2 July 1866)

Although she reacted strongly and negatively to the novel, she found it forceful and wrote to Bentley the next day to reiterate her sentiments: "It will not do you any credit – indeed people will wonder at a House like yours bringing out a work *so ill* calculated for the reading of decent people ... It is just an improper book as bad as any French novel – I entreat you *if* you have made any bargain to *break* it" (BA, Reel 47, 3 July 1866). In her report Jewsbury links the sensation novel with the French novel as it contains what she saw as similar improprieties.

Jewsbury had strong objections to *Not Wisely But Too Well* because of the prominence and immmorality of the love affair. Jewsbury found the novel too sensual and not worthy of publication because the author proclaimed passion as more important than duty. The characters are so overwhelmed by their passion that when they cannot be together, they waste away. Jewsbury did not object to the portrayal of love or passion in novels as long as it was not the center of the novel. She did not want passion to be the goal of a woman's life, a woman's crowning achievement. Broughton agreed to revise it but then she sold the novel to Tinsley. It was Jewsbury's review of this novel that prompted Broughton's literary revenge as mentioned in the Introduction. Although Bentley had not accepted *Not Wisely But Too Well*, he accepted Broughton's second novel, *Cometh up as a Flower* (1867) before he had read Jewsbury's opinion on Broughton, and he published it before the first novel appeared. Jewsbury wrote him; "PS What evil angel persuaded you to accept that coarse vulgar & very objectionable novel Cometh up as a flower? I felt ashamed as I read it" (BA, Reel 47, 20 March 1867). She reviewed *Not Wisely* negatively in the *Athenaeum*, deploring the emphasis on passion. However,

Jewsbury's opinion of Broughton improved over time. She wrote to Bentley in 1874:

> Miss Broughton is as clever as she can stand – very bright & very vivid. & singularly free from false sentiment but in her books she does not recognize any sense of *duty* as per contra inclination. – There is an absence of humanity, more like the genius of Pantomime, where youth & strength & beauty & mutual inclination, *overrides all feeling of compassion* or consideration for that wh is old weak or suffering – or – *ugly*.
>
> There is certainly no *pretence* in her novels & it is therein that she reflects the frank selfishness wh characterise *youth* of the present day – the absence of all traditional reverence or respect. This jars on my taste, to put it at the lowest; – *clever* she is.
>
> So you see I am not unjust to her talents – wh w^d be *genius*, if she put more heart & *soul* into her work. (BA, Reel 46, 9 January 1874)

Jewsbury was disturbed by Broughton's work because she knew the woman had talent, but did not think she applied it correctly. She finds Broughton typical in some ways of a younger generation who lacks respect for tradition. Jewsbury was not in favour of the changing taste in literature towards sensation novels and disliked seeing heroines who behaved badly. Literature was changing and so were women, but not in the way Jewsbury wished.

After reading the first volume of *Under Two Flags* by Ouida, Jewsbury declares that she cannot tell, without reading the whole, if the authoress will redeem her moral; "not much connection to real life": "it is *tricky* & *meretricious* ... with an air of familiarity with mistresses countezens horses gaming drinking swearing driving horseracing idleness cookery – and Barrack slang ... I dare say the story wd *sell* but I think you wd *lower* the *character of yr house if you accept* it"; "it is *not* a story that will do any man or woman or child any good to read it is an *idle* and very immoral book & written on the pattern of French novels It is disgusting for a woman to play with such subject as are treated of – or to speak of them with familiarity". Jewsbury recognized the readability of *Under Two Flags*, but advised Bentley not to accept it: "I can tell you *privately* that the publishers of her last book Strathmore were considered to have *disgraced* themselves by it and they declared that they would never take another – this I heard *privately* so keep it confidential" (BA, Reel 47, 29 December 1865). Jewsbury predicted that the novel would sell, but favoured morality and the reputation of Bentley over money; Bentley refused the novel and lost out on a best-seller. These works by Wood, Braddon, Broughton, and Ouida are still today widely read, entertaining, and indicative of the era.

Fritschner cites Jewsbury as a "hack" reader: "a guardian of convention and morality" (1980: 94); "[w]ith Geraldine Jewsbury it was a priggish personal morality and vision of the moral responsibility of the Bentley firm which guided many of her judgements" (1980: 68). Although Jewsbury approved of happy endings, she did not like someone who had done something wrong to be easily redeemed and end happily. The morally reprehensible should not be rewarded, but should acknowledge their wrongs and live with them. Jewsbury believed that people needed to do their duty and what was right, and consequently she hated attractive pictures of vice. She believed that there was no such thing as a justified adulteress; adultery was immoral. Yet her beliefs were never set in stone; at times she found that a novel was readable and would sell well despite such activities. "With few exceptions Miss Jewsbury's advice kept Bentley on the safe side of public opinion as the publisher of established types of fiction. But it also left him in the rear of the changes taking place in fiction in the 1860s, and this at a time when what was different was still likely to be popular" (Fahnestock, 1973: 271). Jewsbury could not control the drift of what was published. Although she attempted through her work at Bentley and Son to influence the morality of novels published, she was not successful from keeping them from being published, yet she protected the reputation of her employer.

The best novels published reverberated with the character and meaning that she strove to find or instill in the lesser works she reviewed. Part of her difficulty was that she worked for male publishers, under certain guidelines, and could not threaten her own position within this culture. As she saw the situation, women who were not yet able to think for themselves, particularly young women, needed to be educated to become better human beings. As Bianca proclaims in Jewsbury's novel, *The Half Sisters* (1848): "If girls who have been allowed to grow up without unhealthy stimulants can be taken, when their faculties begin to ripen, to see the best performances on the stage, and to hear the best music, it gives an impulse to their intellect, and a development to their ideas that makes their existence and their character stronger and more complete" (1848: 363). And so it was with literature, if the best, or at least healthiest could be provided, it would benefit them.

She sought in the reviews something more than decency, she wanted to show a way for women to better themselves, to not accept a world in which love was all in all and love outside the bonds of marriage was acceptable, and to suggest how women could enjoy life without marriage. Karen M. Carney gives an overview on Jewsbury: "Rather than viewing her career as a publisher's reader as something apart from her work as a novelist or essayist, as other critics have done, it might better be seen as the concluding chapter in a body of work dedicated to women's issues" (1996: 148–49). She "demanded quality, intelligence, and the advocacy of independent thought in books intended for women" (Carney, 1996: 149). Her own novels, her articles, and her book reviews all laid out her intellectual and feminist principles. She continued to believe each educated woman would add to the benefit of society and strove to make each reader better educated.

At the end of her life, Jewsbury suffered from cancer, and she described her condition to Walter Mantell on 14 April 1880: "Since the beginning of this year I have been ill and am so still and likely to be so – or rather no prospect held out of any betternesss – it is a sudden coming on of old age wh seems to have overtaken me all at once & the *settling down* has begun tho' it may continue some time – *writing*, the *act* of writing, has somehow grown strangely difficult, no particular *reason* for it, only the fact!" (Dunn, vol. 8). Jewsbury faced her mortality head on, describing the start of a process that led to her death as "the *settling down*". She continued to see only a few old friends, among whom was George Bentley – and she continued to make reports to him. Jewsbury's last letter to Bentley, written about two weeks before she died, concludes: "And now I grieve to say I am too weak & too ill to *read any more* – sorry I am but I cannot get thro those MS I have in hand" (qtd. Carney, 1996: 155). Her friendship meant much to Bentley: "George Bentley kept this report tucked between the pages of his personal diary, where he recorded this eulogium: 'Few people that I have met summed up a piece of criticism in a humorous dictum better than she did. She was decided, & had the genius of common sense to render decision in her case generally correct. Her kindness, goodness & worth are beyond talking about, & I feel that I love her too much to talk coolly on such points'" (qtd. Carney, 1996: 155). Geraldine Endsor Jewsbury died from cancer on 23 September 1880, aged sixty-eight, at a private hospital in Burwood Place, Edgware Road, London.

Jewsbury could not stem the tide of the changing nature of fiction, but she upheld values of quality and morality in literature that she thought would assist women in leading moral lives. She helped Bentley to position his publishing house as "the leading producer of multi-volume fiction for the libraries" (Sutherland, 1989: 58). Labouring under the weight of the volumes that were submitted and hampered by unacceptable volumes, she worked tirelessly to influence the works that would be read by a generation of women and hoped to guide them through their lives.

CONCLUSION

Jewsbury's Legacy: Jewsbury Today

> We are indications of a development of womanhood which as yet is not recognised. It has, so far, no ready-made channels to run in, but still we have looked, and tried, and found that the present rules for women will not hold us – that something better and stronger is needed.
>
> —Geraldine Jewsbury to Jane Welsh Carlyle ([Undated], Ireland, 1892: 348)

Jewsbury left behind her a large literary legacy and an exemplar for the women who came after her. She saw a problem with gender roles in her day, and in her life and her work Jewsbury attempted to make the world a better place for women by encouraging them to better themselves as individuals. Through her writing she described the limiting conditions for women and children and members of the lower classes prevalent in Victorian society and suggested what could be done to solve the problems. Never taking herself too seriously, Jewsbury wrote to Jane Welsh Carlyle: "I have a great notion that I really am a great fool, without any mitigating features – and so I can judge of wisdom like a disinterested spectator who is not a shareholder" ([12 February 1844], Ireland, 1892: 103). Using her judgment as an anonymous reviewer and publisher's reader, she guided others towards books that would be helpful to them in making better decisions in their lives. Personally, Jewsbury attempted to bring out the best in her friends. She turned her professional acquaintances into friends and always attempted to expand her circle to include people of other generations and servants, developing a supportive community around her.

Jewsbury was overlooked after her death because her books went out of print, the "Carlyle controversy" discredited her reputation, and much of her work remained anonymous. Her letters to Jane Welsh Carlyle were edited and published in 1892; her letters to Walter Mantell remain largely unexplored, although a few scholars have combed them; those to Betta Johnes are unpublished; other letters are scattered in archives around the world, and many are probably still in private hands. According to Jewsbury's biographer, Susanne Howe, her literary executor was John Stores Smith, but he never published any material left in his care. Jewsbury herself was against a biography, writing to Welsh Carlyle: "what would become of us if any superior person were to go and write our 'life and errors'? What a precious mess a 'truthful person' would go and make of us, and how very different to what we really are or were!" ([1849?], Ireland, 1892: 337). Although no one can accurately devise the truth of Jewsbury's life and accomplishments, this study has been an attempt by a "truthful person" to record the importance of her works and ideas.

Few of Jewsbury's shorter works remain in print or are readily available. Dale Spender and Janet Todd Dale published six letters from Jewsbury to Welsh Carlyle in their *British Women Writers* (1989) while Cathy Davidson brought out one letter from Jewsbury to Welsh Carlyle as an example of a love triangle composed of Jewsbury, Thomas Carlyle, and Jane Welsh Carlyle (1992). *The New Beacon Book of Quotations by Women* contains ten quotations from Jewsbury: eight from *Zoe*, two from letters to Welsh Carlyle (Maggio, 1996). In *The Quotable Woman: The First 5,000 Years*

(2011) Elaine Bernstein Partnow gives three quotations from Jewsbury, two from *The Half Sisters* and one from the letters to Welsh Carlyle. A chapter from Jewsbury's *The Sorrows of Gentility* is published by Margaret Beetham and Kay Boardman in 2001 as an example of a serially-published novel in a Victorian women's magazine. Jewsbury's reviews, "Religious Faith and Modern Scepticism" and "Review of 'Adam Bede'", are included in Harriet Devine Jump's *Women's Writing of the Victorian Period* (1999), and Jewsbury's review of *Cometh Up as a Flower* appears in Solveig C. Robinson's collection of literary criticism by women (2003). One of Jewsbury's short stories, "Agnes Lee", is included by Dennis Denisoff in his anthology of Victorian short stories (2004). I have edited a collection of Jewsbury's shorter works, *Leading the Way for Victorian Women: Geraldine Jewsbury and Victorian Culture* (2019). Publications such as these will help to make Jewsbury more available for reading and teaching purposes.

The republication by Virago in the late 1900s of Jewsbury's first two novels (*Zoe*, 1989; *The Half Sisters*, 1994), made those works better known.[1] All of her novels, like her short stories, remain good reading today and could be incorporated into college and graduate classes. Her work is concerned with ideas and social problems of deep interest to feminists and scholars. The novels are long, and yet even the least appealing of them offers insights on important concepts, such as problems of education, class, employment, marriage, spousal abuse, and child abuse – problems that are still too much with us. Foremost, she called on women, and men, to be rational, to consider their situation carefully, to find mentors and friends, to lead useful lives. Throughout her career Jewsbury attempted to guide the choices that women make.

Jewsbury is not now widely read in the university classroom partly because of the length of her novels, the unavailability of her works, and because her work is not well known. Taste in novels has changed since Jewsbury's heyday, but her novels should not be cast aside. Updated publication of her short stories could be a means of making her work more available to teachers. The tradition of canon formation has excluded women from the start and women's contributions to literature are frequently undervalued. Professors tend to teach what they were taught, or works they know, and what is readily available, hence, many overlook Jewsbury. In recent decades some changes have been made in the anthologies traditionally taught in college classes, primarily those published by Norton, Oxford, and Longman, but these do not as yet include Jewsbury. One tendency in recent years, to include more untraditional genres within anthologies such as reviews and letters, may offer another path to make Jewsbury more widely known. For example, Anne-Marie Beller received a Curran Fellowship to research Jewsbury's *Athenaeum* reviews. Increased scholarly work on Jewsbury will provide greater knowledge of her work, leading to a larger readership. Making her work more widely known, more available, and consequently more frequently discussed by scholars, can change the current status of Jewsbury's work. As John Sutherland proclaimed, Jewsbury is the "most accomplished all-round lady of letters of the nineteenth century" (2009). Yet there is not enough recognition of her unique and eminent position within Victorian literature and culture.

One difficulty with Jewsbury's work is with the sheer amount of material and the different genres in which Jewsbury wrote. Although her novels are well spoken of, they have not been placed on that top tier that Jewsbury had aspired to when she published *Zoe*. There is no greatest accomplishment that shines out from the many she achieved. She worked but always had time for other people. Perhaps she was too much like us. Susanne Howe sums up Jewsbury by stating: "Her great distinction seems to have been merely this, that she was herself, supremely and whole-heartedly, during a period in English life when that was a difficult and rare achievement for a woman" (1935: 201). She was not always a "good" feminist, but who is? Roxane Gay points out the dissension among feminists today of what it means to be a feminist; "If I am, indeed, a feminist, I am a rather bad one. I am a mess of contradictions" (2014: 373). Jewsbury felt differently at diverse times and her thoughts changed over the years, as is the case for all of us, but she spoke honestly in the moment. What Jewsbury wrote to her friend Walter Mantell about relationships, could be said of all her beliefs; "none of us know whither we are going – but if we are *true*, we shall come true in spite of *seeming* inconsistencies & contradictions" (Dunn, vol. 2, 27 May 1857). Jewsbury was flawed and human, but always scintillating company in person and in her work. She speaks to us today because her concerns were much like ours: she tackles the basic problem of how to live our lives. Always concerned with living an ethical life, in her works she brought up important questions and described the problems within Victorian society, in her life she created relationships of equality and always supported those on the outskirts of society.

Writing, whether writing fiction, non-fiction, or letters, was the center of Jewsbury's life. Although disappointed by not marrying, she made the most of her life as a single woman and she found writing a relief from her life; "When I am much annoyed, or have done anything foolish … my first impulse is always to cut my throat, and the next, to set to work savagely, and it is surprising how soon one gets into a state of indifference!" (6 October 1851, Ireland, 1892: 425). Writing took Jewsbury outside of her individual life and allowed her to use her experiences to inform others. She found her own voice and encouraged other women to express themselves.

In all of her work, Jewsbury battles with the issues identified by Virginia Woolf in her lecture, "Professions for Women", given in 1931. The daughter of Victorian parents, Woolf still wrestled with the conventions of that earlier era, just as Jewsbury struggled with them during the era itself. Woolf describes the Angel in the House: "She was intensely sympathetic. She was immensely charming. She was utterly unselfish. She excelled in the difficult arts of family life. She sacrificed herself daily" (1942), and posits that a woman writer needs to kill the Angel in the House in herself. The strictures of the Angel were the "present rules for women" that Jewsbury wrote to Jane Welsh Carlyle "will not hold us" ([Undated], Ireland, 1892: 348). Jewsbury's generation could not break entirely free. Jewsbury had shaken off the fear of entering the public sphere when she began to publish, but she thought the effort had made her "hard", and she grappled with the idea of the woman she thought she should be and the person she was. That Woolf was able to strangle the Angel is due to the channels forged by the generation before her and the work of women like Jewsbury. Today we still struggle with the idea of what women ought to be.

Woolf faced her second hurdle as a writer when she "thought of something, something about the body, about the passions which it was unfitting for a woman to say. Men, her reason told her, would be shocked" (1942). This expression of feelings and passions was something that the Angel in the House never expressed. But Jewsbury was a passionate woman and spoke her thoughts openly. Her first two novels shocked the public with their exposure of social problems, private conflicts, and unfulfilled passions. Susanne Howe comments that Jewsbury's lack of reticence in her letters leads to a perception of her lack of subtlety (1966: 238). Her letters show her devotion to her friends and her inclusiveness towards others. Her letters do not contain well-constructed amusing stories like those of Welsh Carlyle. They contain her thoughts of the moment as they jump from topic to topic, but they can illuminate those topics as well. In some ways they are like her novels, not tightly constructed, but they are endowed with spots of brilliance and spots of the ordinary which afford their own pleasure in showing how this singular woman approached her life.

Although Jewsbury was never able to escape the sense that being without a mother made her hard and that she should be more like the Angel in the House, she accomplished something important with her life and writings. She saw, as she wrote to Welsh Carlyle, that the women of the future would go beyond what she and Welsh Carlyle had accomplished in their lives. She felt that she had made a start, but there was much more to do. She had traveled in a path indicated by her sister, Maria Jane Jewsbury, but went much further along that path. Everything she wrote was geared for the betterment of women. She longed for women to be better educated, to be better employed, and she was optimistic about the future. Although there was no "ready-made channel" for Jewsbury to follow in her life and career, she created a channel for women of the future.

Notes

Chapter 1. Early Influences: Becoming Geraldine Jewsbury

1. The Wordsworth Trust gives "woeful" but is unsure of the transcription. Clarke gives "wonderful" (1990: 72), indicating that Maria Jane is writing about Jewsbury's imagination and not her penmanship.
2. Maria Jane Jewsbury contributed over seventy items to thirteen different annuals. One critic comments: "Regarding the annuals, no doubt, as a steady source of income, Miss Jewsbury conformed to the accepted pattern: her poems and stories savour of the propriety and refinement required from annuals intended as ornaments for the drawing-room table and would not have given offence to the most fastidious mind. Consequently, her contributions betray little of the original mind and satirical vein displayed in *Phantasmagoria* and *The Three Histories* …" (qtd. Fryckstedt, 1984: 201–02).
3. In her own despair, Anna Brownell Jameson had published *The Diary of an Ennuyée* (1826), a novel written as if by a young woman who travels through Europe suffering from melancholia from an undisclosed cause and who finally dies. The word "*ennuyé*" appears frequently in Jewsbury's second novel *The Half Sisters* (1848), which addresses in more depth than her first novel, *Zoe*, the problem of the middle-class woman who has nothing to do.
4. In her dissertation Rosenmayer (1970) prints Jewsbury's letters to Thomas Carlyle from a transcription made by Susanne Howe who owned the originals which are now housed in the Alexander Turnbull Library, Wellington, New Zealand.
5. "Greenheys derived its name from De Quincey's old home, 'Green hay,' a picturesque house in the neighbourhood, surrounded by extensive grounds. It was built by De Quincey's father in 1791. The house has long ago been demolished, but the site can be pointed out to his devotees, though the generation that remembers it is fast passing away. Not far from the Pepperhill Farm lived Geraldine Jewsbury with her brother, in Carlton Terrace" (Chadwick, 1910: 235).
6. Genius concerns breaking free of bonds and not conforming to the expectations of the day. John Evans frequently describes Jewsbury as a genius in *Lancashire Authors and Orators* published in 1850. J. M. Hartley considers the manner in which Jewsbury uses the term: "By genius … Jewsbury seems to have

had in mind the relatively modern meaning, given by the O.E.D. as in use from the middle of the eighteenth century: 'native intellectual power of an exalted type, such as is attributed to those who are esteemed greatest in any department of art, speculation or practice: instinctive or extraordinary capacity for imaginative creation, original thought, invention or discovery'" (1979: 149 n. 9). The expression "woman of genius" was applied in many ways at the time. Clarke suggests that the term "was well established by the 1840s as a pejorative term indicating a woman who demanded more attention than was good for her"; Thomas Carlyle describes his mother-in-law, a woman he had very little patience with, as such, telling his wife: "Your mother, my Dear, has narrowly missed being a woman of genius'" (Clarke, 1990: 148).

Chapter 2. The Carlyles and *Zoe*: Discovering the World

1. This passage is pointed out by Rosenmayer (1973: 13).
2. Mrs. Elizabeth (Betsey) Paulet was the eldest daughter of the Wesleyan Methodist preacher Robert Newton, married to a Swiss businessman, and living at Seaforth House, four miles from Liverpool, built by John Gladstone (CLO, TC to JWC, 19 July 1841, Note 4). Elizabeth Paulet was to publish her own novel *Dharma, Or Three Phases of Love* in 1865. *Dharma* has many characteristics and themes in common with *Zoe* which perhaps indicate that Paulet used material she thought about for the joint novel for her independent endeavour. Like Zoe, Paulet's heroine is a well-educated, beautiful woman from another culture. There are lengthy philosophical discussions in the novel. Much of the interaction involves Protestants and Catholics and addresses the marrying of priests, a theme that interested Jewsbury. The novel is also concerned with the fighting for freedom in Italy as Paulet, like Jewsbury, was influenced by Giuseppe Mazzini. Jewsbury concluded her review of *Dharma* in the *Athenaeum* with this sentence: "Incoherent and foolish as the story is, there are evidences of talent in the book which make us wish that so much labour had been bestowed on a more rational subject" (*Athenaeum*, 10 June 1865: 777).

Chapter 3. Fiction and Short Pieces: Educating Readers

1. Scholars have suggested that Bianca is based on Madame de Staël's heroine Corinne, as well as the actress Charlotte Cushman, who was a friend of Jewsbury's. Around 1877 Jewsbury wrote a reminiscence of Cushman printed by Emma Stebbins with excerpts from Jewsbury's letters to Cushman. Alice is sometimes seen as a portrait of Jane Welsh Carlyle (Clarke, 1990: 188) who is thought to have considered running away with a man who was not her husband.
2. Miss Airlie excites "a romantic emotion" (Jewsbury, 1853: 349) that is described similarly to the feelings Jewsbury expressed for Welsh Carlyle.
3. In Molière's *George Dandin ou le Mari Confondu* (1668), the peasant Dandin marries a woman from a higher class who is unfaithful to him. He mutters this phrase, literally "you wanted it", indicating that he has only himself to blame.

Chapter 4. Letters: Jane Welsh Carlyle, Walter Mantell, and Other Friendships

1. Jewsbury's letters written between 1841 and 1852 to Jane Welsh Carlyle were published by Mrs. Alexander Ireland. Approximately five hundred letters written to Walter Mantell from 1851 and 1880 are housed at the Alexander Turnbull Library, Wellington, New Zealand; these were transcribed by Waldo H. Dunn and are held at Ohio State University. Letters written to members of the Johnes family from 1861 to 1880 are housed in the National Library of Wales.
2. Jewsbury records that she has undertaken to learn capitals and stops and grammar for the benefit of her publications (Ireland, 1892: 121–22). Jane Welsh Carlyle attempted to help her but had to stop, because, as she wrote to John Forster, her husband "has got some furious objection to my meddling with them – even declares I 'don't know bad grammar when I see it any better than *she* does'" (CLO, 20 November 1847). At a later date Jewsbury requests that Walter Mantell correct proofs for her: "*do not* be *sparing* cut off all superfluities & redundant words & sentences … dear me you know Latin & Greek & every thing else & I know nothing at all about those occult branches of humanity especially grammar & spelling – one thing please, if any expression strikes you as being in bad taste – take it out *leave nothing in, you dislike*" (Dunn, vol. 2, 11 July 1857).
3. A comparison of Ireland's transcription of Jewsbury's letter (Ireland, 1892: 219) and the transcription made by Charles William Sutton (author of the DNB entry on Jewsbury) held by the Manchester Central Library shows *many* changes and omissions. In addition, Rosenmayer discusses the inaccuracy of Mrs. Ireland's dating of many of the letters (1973: 13 and following). Librarian Johannes E. Andersen at the Alexander Turnbull Library in Wellington, New Zealand wrote to Susanne Howe on 28 August 1935 about Mantell's copy of Ireland's book of Jewsbury's letters to Welsh Carlyle: "I have a copy in which Mr Mantell has numbered the peppered blanks through the volume where Mrs I. [Ireland] has omitted the names referred by Miss J., and I thought maybe the numbers belonged to a key of the names; but there is no such key. Mr Mantell evidently numbering the blanks to count up how many people the young lady had something to say about!"
4. Some commentators, such as Lillian Mohin and Anna Wilson view Geraldine Jewsbury as one of the *Past Participants in Lesbianism* (1984). Faderman sees the relationship as "charged with a warmth, a fervor, a passion that went beyond simple friendship" (1981: 51–52). S. Marcus claims Jewsbury was "more interested in relationships with women than in marriage to men" (2009: 204).
5. There is little tradition of women proposing to men until about 1900 when it became more frequent, at least as can be judged by the frequency of magazine articles on the topic.

Chapter 5. Jewsbury as a Reviewer and Editor: Forwarding the Cause of Women

1. Roberts (2005) lists the following scholars in this category: Fryckstedt, 1986: 37; Showalter, 1977: 177; Fritschner, 1980: 94.
2. According to Monica Correa Fryckstedt the marked file is housed in the Special Collections, City University, London (1986: 9).
3. There is a Jewsbury family story that Jewsbury suggested rejection of the manuscript of *Alice in Wonderland* while working for Bentley and Son, but it has not been substantiated (letter from George J. Binns to Mrs. Noble, 22 July 1935).

Chapter 6. Jewsbury as a Publisher's Reader: Reading for Women

1. Published by Bentley and Son in 1859. This was a precursor to the memoirs Jewsbury worked on and saw through publication after Lady Morgan's death.
2. Arthur Wellesley, 2nd Duke of Wellington 1807–84, soldier and politician, eldest son of the victor of Waterloo and Prime Minister; Charles Pelham Villiers 1802–98, British lawyer and politician.

Conclusion. Jewsbury's Legacy: Jewsbury Today

1. Most scholars believe Jewsbury's first two novels are her best: Jeanne Rosenmayer (1970) thinks *The Sorrows of Gentility* (1856) is her greatest novel, while Eleanor Langstaff (1989) prefers *Marian Withers* (1851).

Bibliography

1. Works by Geraldine Jewsbury

1845 [1989], *Zoe*. London: Virago.

1846a, "To-Day", *Douglas Jerrold's Shilling Magazine* 3 (March): 223–25. HathiTrust. Accessed: 24 March 2017.

1846b, "The Present and the Future", *Douglas Jerrold's Shilling Magazine* 3 (June): 543–48. HathiTrust. Accessed: 27 March 2017.

1846c, "Social Barbarisms. Hiring a Servant", *Douglas Jerrold's Shilling Magazine* 4 (November): 462–71. HathiTrust. Accessed: 27 March 2017.

1847a, "How Agnes Worral Was Taught to be Respectable", *Douglas Jerrold's Shilling Magazine* 5 (January): 16–24. HathiTrust. Accessed: 3 March 2017.

1847b, "How Agnes Worral Was Taught to be Respectable. Some Account of the Life Agnes Lead with the Two Old Ladies to Whom She Was Sent to Learn Proper Behaviour", *Douglas Jerrold's Shilling Magazine* 5 (March): 246–66. HathiTrust. Accessed: 3 March 2017.

1847c, "The Lower Orders", *Douglas Jerrold's Shilling Magazine* 5 (April): 362–67. HathiTrust. Accessed: 3 March 2017.

1847d, "Civilisation of the 'Lower Orders'", *Douglas Jerrold's Shilling Magazine* 6 (November): 443–52. HathiTrust. Accessed: 3 March 2017.

1848 [1994], *The Half Sisters*. Oxford: Oxford University Press.

1850a, "Religious Faith and Modern Scepticism", *Westminster Review* 50 (January): 379–407.

1850b, "The Young Jew of Tunis". *Household Words* (27 April): 118–20. DJO. Accessed: 29 July 2017.

1851, *Marian Withers*, London: Colburn and Co., Publishers.

1852a, "A Forgotten Celebrity". *Household Words* (28 February 1852): 534–38. DJO. Accessed: 29 July 2017.

1852b, "The Story of Angelique. (A True Incident.)", *Ladies Companion Magazine* (May 1852): 225–31. HathiTrust. Accessed: 29 July 2017.

1853, *The History of an Adopted Child*. (London: Grant and Griffith). Google Books. Accessed: 15 June 2017.

1855a, *Angelo; or, the Pine Forest in the Alps*. London: Grant and Griffith. Google Books. Accessed: 1 July 2017.

1855b, *Constance Herbert*. 3 vols. London: Hurst and Blackett, Publishers.
1855c, "Specimens of the Alchemists", *Household Words* (June 16): 457–65. DJO. Accessed: 29 July 2017.
1855d, "Tardy Justice", *Household Words* (27 October): 298–301. DJO. Accessed: 29 July 2017.
1856 [1864], *The Sorrows of Gentility*. 2nd ed. 2 vols. London: Chapman and Hall, 1864. Google Books. Accessed: 19 June 2017.
1857, "Agnes Lee", *Household Words* (11 July): 36–46. DJO. Accessed: 29 July 2017.
1859a, "Nicholas the Rope-Dancer", *Household Words* (21 May): 588–594. DJO. Accessed: 29 July 2017.
1859b, *Right or Wrong*. 2 vols. London: Hurst and Blackett, Publishers. Google Books. Accessed: 1 July 2017.
1861, "Medieval Sketches". *Victoria Regia*. Adelaide A. Procter (ed.). London: Victoria Press: 85–94.
1876, "Introduction." *Memoir and Correspondence of Caroline Herschel*. Mrs. John Herschel. London, John Murray. A Celebration of Women Writers. U Penn. digital.library.upenn.edu/women/herschel/memoir/memoir.html. Accessed: 15 August 2017.

2. Reviews in the Athenaeum by Geraldine Jewsbury

25 March 1854, *Books for Children*: 373–74.
24 June 1854, *Hide and Seek*, by W. Wilkie Collins: 775.
18 November 1854, *Heartsease; or the Brother's Wife*, by [Charlotte Mary Yonge]: 1397.
27 January 1855, *The Warden*, by Anthony Trollope: 107.
14 July 1855, *A Letter to the Queen on Lord Chancellor Cranworth's Bill*, by the Hon. Mrs. Norton, and *Women in the Nineteenth Century; and Kindred Papers Relating to the Sphere, Condition, and Duties of Woman*, by Margaret Fuller Ossoli: 811–12.
14 June 1856, *Hertha*, by Fredrika Bremer: 739.
14 March 1857, *The Feminine Soul: its Nature and Attributes*, by Elizabeth Strutt: 341.
5 June 1858, *Intellectual Education, and its Influence on the Character and Happiness of Women*, by Emily Shirreff: 714–15.
18 September 1858, *Woman, her Mission and her Life*, by Adolphe Monod: 360.
26 February 1859, *Adam Bede*, by George Eliot: 284.
26 March 1859, *The Bertrams: a Novel*, by Anthony Trollope: 420.
9 July 1859, *The Ordeal of Richard Feverel*, by George Meredith: 48.
20 August 1859, *Out of the Depths: the Story of a Woman's Life*: 240–41.
14 April 1860, *Woman's Right to Labour or, Low Wages and Hard Work*, by Caroline Dall: 504.
14 July 1860, *Chapters on Wives*, by Mrs. Ellis: 52–53.
25 August 1860, *Englishwomen and the Age*, by Mrs. Horace Roscoe St. John: 248–50.

24 November 1860, *My Life, and What Shall I Do with IT? A Question for Young Gentlewomen*, by an Old Maid: 702–03.
7 December 1861, *Lovel the Widower*, by W. M. Thackeray: 758.
19 July 1862, *Mrs. Beeton's Book of Household Management*: 78–79.
2 August 1862, *Woman: What She Has Been, What She Is, What She Will Be, or What She Ought to Be*, by J. T. L.: 139.
25 April 1863, *The Story of Elizabeth*, by [Anne Thackeray]: 552.
30 May 1863, *A Dark Night's Work*, by Mrs. Gaskell: 708.
11 July 1863, *Romola*, by George Eliot: 46.
21 May 1864, *Diaries of a Lady of Quality, from 1797 to 1844*, by A. Hayward (ed.): 705–06.
1 October 1864, *The Maori King; or, the Story of our Quarrel with the Natives of New Zealand*, by J. E. Gorst: 423–25.
10 June 1865, *Dharma; or, Three Phases of Love*, by E. Paulet: 777.
17 February 1866, *Woman Against Woman*, by Florence Marryat: 233.
24 November 1866, *A Brief Essay on the Position of Women*, by Mrs. C. H. Spear: 674–75.
20 April 1867, *Cometh up a Flower: An Autobiography*, by [Rhoda Broughton]: 514–15.
15 February 1868, *Under Two Flags: A Story of the Household and the Desert*, by Ouidà: 248–49.
21 March 1868, *Charlotte's Inheritance: a Novel*, by [Mary Elizabeth Braddon]: 418.
26 December 1868, *Studious Women*, by Monseigneur Dupanloup: 881–82.
31 July 1869, *Woman's Work and Woman's Culture: a Series of Essays*, by Josephine E. Butler (ed.): 135–36.
6 August 1870, *The Life of Madame de Beauharnais de Miramion, 1629–1696*, by M. Alfred Bonnear: 170–72.

3. Manuscripts, Edited Works, and Letters of Geraldine Jewsbury

Bloom, Abigail Burnham, (ed.), 2019. *Leading the Way for Victorian Women: Geraldine Jewsbury and Victorian Culture*. Edward Everett Root Publishers Co. Ltd.

Dunn, Waldo H., transcriptions of the letters of GEJ to Walter Mantel, 8 volumes, Ohio State University Libraries Special Collections, SPEC.RARE.CMS.46.

Ireland, Mrs. Alexander, (ed.), 1892. *Selections from the Letters of Geraldine Endsor Jewsbury to Jane Welsh Carlyle*. London: Longmans, Green, and Co.

Jewsbury, Geraldine, letters, Mantell Family Papers, Alexander Turnbull Library, Wellington, New Zealand. MS-Copy-Micro-0483–22 to MS-Copy-Micro-0488–25.

___, letters to Betha Johnes, National Library of Wales, Dolaucothi Estate Records. L7076–7134.

___, letters to Lewald-Stahr, Nachl. Lewald-Stahr, K. 15, Nr. 313, Staatsbibliothek zu Berlin.

___, letters to Messrs. Chapman and Hall, 1844–48. Literary and Historical Manuscripts, Morgan Library. Record ID 104760.

___, letter to Mr Sydenham Nodes[?], 21 July 1851, William Hepworth Dixon Papers, 1845–79, Special Collections, University of California, Los Angeles. Box 1.

___, letters to William Hepworth Dixon, 25 February 1856 and 1 October 1861, William Hepworth Dixon Papers, 1845–79, Special Collections, University of California, Los Angeles. Box 1.

___, letter to William H. Dixon, 21 April 1862, Beinecke Rare Book and Manuscript Library, Yale University. GEN MSS MISC William Hepworth Dixon Papers.

Sutton, Charles W., transcription of letter of GEJ to JWC, Archives & Local History, Manchester Central Library. MSC 920/J (Jewsbury).

4. Other Sources

Adichie, Chimamanda Ngozi, 2012. "We should all be feminists" (Dec. 2012 TED talk). https://www.ted.com/talks/chimamanda_ngozi_adichie_we_should_all_be_feminists/transcript#t-779379. Accessed: 3 April 2018.

Ahmed, Sara, 2017. *Living a Feminist Life*. Durham: Duke University Press. Kindle.

Andersen, Johannes E., letter to Susanne Howe, 28 August 1935. In the possession of the author.

Atkinson, Juliette, 2017. *French Novels and the Victorians*. Oxford: Oxford University Press.

Barker, Juliet, 1994. *The Brontës*. New York: St. Martin's Press.

Beetham, Margaret, and Kay Boardman, (eds.), 2001. *Victorian Women's Magazines: An Anthology*. Manchester: Manchester University Press, 2001: 32–35.

[Bentley Archives, BA]. The Archives of Richard Bentley and Son, 1829–98, 116 reels, Cambridge, England: Chadwick-Healey, 1976; Teaneck, NJ: Somerset House, 1976.

Binns, George J., letter to Mrs. Noble, 22 July 1935. In the possession of the author.

Broughton, Rhoda, 1894. *A Beginner*. New York: D. Appleton and Company. Google Books. Accessed: 2 February 2017.

Calder, Jenni, 1976. *Women and Marriage in Victorian Fiction*. London: Thames and Hudson.

Carlyle, Thomas, and Jane Welsh Carlyle. *The Carlyle Letters Online* [CLO]. Brent E. Kinser (ed.). (Duke University Press, 2007–2016). www.carlyleletters.org. Accessed: 21 January 2017.

Carney, Karen M., 1996. "The Publisher's Reader as Feminist: The Career of Geraldine Endsor Jewsbury", *Victorian Periodicals Review* 29.2 (Summer), 146–58.

Cary, Meredith, 1974. "Geraldine Jewsbury and the Woman Question", *Research Studies* 42.4, 201–14.

Casey, Ellen Miller, 1996. "Edging Women Out?: Reviews of Women Novelists in the *Athenaeum*, 1860–1900", *Victorian Studies* 39.2 (Winter), 151–71.

Chadwick, Mrs. Ellis H, 1910. *Mrs. Gaskell: Haunts, Homes, and Stories*. London: Sir Isaac Pitman and Sons, Ltd.

Chattman, Lauren, 1994. "Actresses at Home and on Stage", *Novel* 28.1 (Fall), 72–89.

Chorley, H. F. 1845. Review of *Zoe, Athenaeum* 901, 1 February 1845, 114.

Clarke, Norma, 1990. *Ambitious Heights: Writing, Friendship, Love—The Jewsbury Sisters, Felicia Hemans, and Jane Welsh Carlyle*. London: Routledge.

Connor, Helene, 2001. "Nineteenth Century Mancunian Novelist and Literary Critic, Geraldine Endsor Jewsbury (1812–1880) and Her Connections with Aotearoa/New Zealand". issuu.com/newobjectlessons/docs/geraldine_endsor_jewsbury. Accessed: 10 June 2013.

Cott, Nancy, 1987. *The Grounding of Modern Feminism*. New Haven and London: Yale University Press.

Cruikshank, Margaret, 1979. "Geraldine Jewsbury and Jane Carlyle", *Frontiers: A Journal of Women Studies* 4.3, *Lesbian History* (Autumn): 60–64.

Dames, Nicholas, 2009. "On the Protocols of Victorian Citation", *Novel* 42.2 (Summer): 326–33. ProQuest. Accessed: 20 July 2017.

Davidson, Cathy N., (ed.), 1992. *The Book of Love: Writers and their Love Letters*. New York: Pocket Books.

Denisoff, Dennis, (ed.), 2004. *The Broadview Anthology of Victorian Short Stories*. Peterborough: Broadview. 163–85.

Dixon, Ella Hepworth, 1930. *"As I Knew Them": Sketches of People I Have Met on the Way*. London: Hutchinson.

Easley, Alexis. 2011. *Literary Celebrity, Gender, and Victorian Authorship 1850–1914*. Newark: University of Delaware Press.

Ellis, Mrs. [Sarah Stickney], 1839. *The Women of England: Their Social Duties, and Domestic Habits*. London: Fisher, Son, & Co. Haithitrust. Accessed: 28 September 2019.

Espinasse, Francis, 1893. *Literary Recollections and Sketches*. London: Hodder and Stoughton. Google Books. Accessed: 29 April 2016.

Evans, John, 1850. *Lancashire Authors and Orators: A Series of Literary Sketches*. London: Houlston and Stoneman. Google Books. Accessed: 8 May 2018.

Faderman, Lillian, 1981. *Surpassing the Love of Man: Romantic Friendship and Love between Women from the Renaissance to the Present*. New York: William Morrow.

Fahnestock, Jeanne Rosenmayer, 1973. "Geraldine Jewsbury: The Power of the Publisher's Reader", *Nineteenth-Century Fiction* 28.3 (December): 253–72. Jstor. Accessed: 15 December 2017.

Foster, Shirley, 1985. *Victorian Women's Fictions: Marriage, Freedom and the Individual*. Totowa: Barnes & Noble Books.

___, 1989. "Introduction", to *Zoe* by Geraldine Jewsbury. London: Virago: 5–12.

Fox, Caroline, 1882. *Memories of Old Friends: Being Extracts from the Journals of Caroline Fox of Penjerrick, Cornwall from 1835 to 1871*. Horace N. Pym (ed.). London: Smith, Elder.

Fritschner, Linda Marie, 1980. "Publishers' Readers, Publishers, and Their Authors", *Publishing History* 7: 45–100.

Froude, James Anthony, 1903. *My Relations with Carlyle*. New York: Charles Scribner's Sons.

Fryckstedt, Monica Correa, 1983. "New Sources on Geraldine Jewsbury and the Woman Question", *Research Studies* 51, 2: 51–59.

___, 1984. "The Hidden Rill: The Life and Career of Maria Jane Jewsbury: I", *Bulletin of the John Rylands Library* 66, 2: 177–203.

___, 1985. "Geraldine Jewsbury and *Douglas Jerrold's Shilling Magazine*", *English Studies* 66, 4: 326–37.

___, 1986. *Geraldine Jewsbury's Athenaeum Reviews: A Mirror of Mid-Victorian Attitudes to Fiction*. Stockholm.

Gay, Roxane, 2014. *Bad Feminist: Essays*. New York: HarperCollins.

Gettmann, Royal A., 1960. *A Victorian Publisher: A Study of the Bentley Papers*. Cambridge: Cambridge University Press.

Gilbert, Sandra, and Susan Gubar, 1979. *The Mad Woman in the Attic: The Woman Writer and the Nineteenth Century Literary Imagination*. New Haven: Yale University Press.

Gillett, Eric, 1932. *Maria Jane Jewsbury: Occasional Papers, selected with a Memoir*. London: Oxford University Press.

Greg, W. R., 1869. *Why Are Women Redundant?*. London: N. Trübner & Co.

Griest, Guinevere L., 1970. *Mudie's Circulating Library and the Victorian Novel*. Bloomington and London: Indiana University Press.

Hall, S. C., 1883. *Retrospect of a Long Life: From 1815–1883*. New York: D. Appleton and Company.

Hartley, J. M., 1979. "Geraldine Jewsbury and the Problems of the Woman Novelist", *Women's Studies International Quarterly* 2, 2: 137–53.

Howe, Susanne, 1935. *Geraldine Jewsbury: Her Life and Errors*. London: George Allen & Unwin.

___, 1966. *Wilhelm Meister and his English Kinsmen: Apprentices to Life*. 1930. New York: AMS Press: 238–61.

Jeaffreson, John Cordy, 1893. *A Book of Recollections*. 2 vols. HathiTrust. Accessed: 13 December 2017.

Jewsbury, Maria Jane, 1835. *Letters to the Young*. New York: D. Appleton & Co.

___, letters, Special Collections, The John Rylands Library, The University of Manchester. Uncatalogued English MS 1320.

___, letters, transcribed, The Wordsworth Trust. Online. Accessed: 7 May 2017.

Jump, Harriet Devine, 1999a. "'My Dearest Geraldine': Maria Jane Jewsbury's Letters", *Bulletin of the John Rylands University Library of Manchester* 81, 1 (Spring): 62–72.

Jump, Harriet Devine, (ed.), 1999b. *Women's Writing of the Victorian Period 1837–1901: An Anthology*. New York: St. Martin's Press, 62–67; 114–16.

Langstaff, Eleanor, 1989. "Jewsbury, Geraldine", in *British Women Writers: A Critical*

Reference Guide, Janet Todd (ed.), New York: Continuum/Frederick Ungar: 361–62.
Leighton, Angela, and Margaret Reynolds (eds.), 1995. *Victorian Women Poets: An Anthology*. Oxford: Blackwell.
[Lewes, G. H.], 1850. "A Gentle Hint to Writing Women", *Leader* 1: 189.
Lewis, Linda, 2003. *Germaine de Staël, George Sand, and the Victorian Woman Artist*. Columbia: University of Missouri Press.
Maggio, Rosalie, (ed.), 1996. *The New Beacon Book of Quotations by Women*. Boston: Beacon, 1996.
Marcus, Julia, 2000. *Across an Untried Sea: Discovering Lives Hidden in the Shadow of Convention and Time*. New York: Alfred A. Knopf.
Marcus, Sharon, 2009. *Between Women: Friendship, Desire, and Marriage in Victorian England*. Princeton: Princeton University Press.
Martin, Helena Saville Faucit, 1885 [1889]. *On Some of Shakespeare's Female Characters*. 6th ed. Edinburgh and London: William Blackwood and Sons.
Mohin, Lillian, and Anna Wilson, 1984. *Past Participants in Lesbianism* (a diary produced by the Only Women's Press in 1984), Lesbian Gay Bisexual Trans History Month. http://www.lgbthistorymonth.org.uk/history/pastparticipants.htm. Accessed: 1 May 2018.
Morgan, Lady Sydney, 1863. *Lady Morgan's Memoirs—Autobiography, Diaries and Correspondence*. 3 vols. London: W. H. Allen & Co.
"Obituary", 1880. *Times* [London, England] 25 September, 9, *The Times Digital Archive*. Accessed: 23 February 2017.
Oliphant, Mrs., and F. R. Oliphant, 1892. *The Victorian Age of English Literature*. 2 vols. London: Percival and Co.
Partnow, Elaine Bernstein, (comp. and ed.), 2011. *The Quotable Woman: The First 5,000 Years*. Rev. ed. New York: Facts on file/Infobase.
Pope, Catherine, 2013. "Woman Against Woman – Florence Marryat vs Geraldine Jewsbury", www.academia.edu/1669427/Woman_Against_Woman_-_Florence_Marryat_vs_Geraldine_Jewsbury, 10 June 2013. Accessed: 1 May 2018.
Procter, Adelaide, letter to Bessie Rayner Parkes, 7 August 1861. Personal Papers of Bessie Rayner Parkes, Girton College Archive. GCPP Parkes 8/22.
Ray, Gordon N., 1952. "The Bentley Papers", *The Library* s5-VII.3 (1 September): 178–200.
Rendall, Jane, 1985. *The Origins of Modern Feminism: Women in Britain, France and the United States 1780–1860*. Chicago: Lyceum Books.
Roberts, Lewis C., 2005. "The Production of a Female Hand: Professional Writing and the Career of Geraldine Jewsbury", *Womens Writing* 12.3: 399–418.
___, 2016. "The Critical Response to Children's Books in Geraldine Jewsbury's *Athenaeum* Reviews", *Nineteenth-Century Prose* 43, 1/2 (Spring/Fall): 151–70.
Robinson, Solveig C. (ed.), 2003. *A Serious Occupation: Literary Criticism by Victorian Women Writers*. Peterborough: Broadview.
Rosen, Judith, 1996. "At Home upon a Stage: Domesticity and Genius in Geraldine

Jewsbury's *The Half-sisters* (1848)", in Barbara Leah Harman and Susan Meyer (eds.), *The New Nineteenth Century: Feminist Readings of Underread Victorian Fiction*. New York: Garland:17–32.

Rosenmayer, Jeanne, 1970. "Geraldine Jewsbury: Novelist and Publisher's Reader", Diss. University of London, July.

Showalter, Elaine, 1977. *A Literature of Their Own*. Princeton: Princeton University Press.

Solnit, Rebecca, 2017. *The Mother of All Questions*. Chicago: Haymarket Books.

"*The Sorrows of Gentility* by Geraldine Jewsbury", Review, *Athenaeum* (31 May 1856): 675. Hathitrust. Accessed: 1 March 2018.

Spender, Dale, and Janet Todd, (eds.), 1989. *British Women Writers: An Anthology from the Fourteenth Century to the Present*. New York: Peter Bedrick: 471–84.

Stedman, Gesa, 2011. "Passion and Talent, Fulfillment or Death? Germaine de Staël's Novel *Corinne* Crosses the Channel" in *Readers, Writers, Salonnières: Female Networks in Europe, 1700–1900*, Gillian Dow (ed.). New York: Peter Lang: 201–15.

Surridge, Lisa, 1995. "Madame de Stael Meets Mrs. Ellis: Geraldine Jewsbury's *The Half Sisters*", *Carlyle Studies Annual*: 81–95.

Sutherland, John, 1989. *The Stanford Companion to Victorian Fiction*. Stanford: Stanford University Press.

___, 2009. "Jewsbury, Geraldine E[ndsor]". *Longman Companion to Victorian Literature*. Abington, Oxon: Routledge.

Thackeray, W. M., 1847–48 [1994]. *Vanity Fair*. New York, London: W. W. Norton & Company.

Thomson, Patricia, 1997. *George Sands and the Victorians: Her Influence and Reputation in Nineteenth-Century England*. London: Macmillan.

Vicinus, Martha, 1985. *Independent Women: Work & Community for Single Women 1850–1920*. Chicago: University of Chicago Press.

___, 2004. *Intimate Friends: Women Who Loved Women, 1778–1928*. Chicago: University of Chicago Press.

Werner, Mary B., and Kenneth Womack, 1997. "Forbidden Love and Victorian Restraint in Geraldine Jewsbury's Zoe", *Cahiers Victoriens et Edouardiens* 45: 15–25.

Wilkes, Joann, 1988. "Walter Mantell, Geraldine Jewsbury, and Race Relations in New Zealand", *New Zealand Journal of History* 22, 2: 105–17.

___, 1994. "Introduction", *The Half Sisters: A Tale* by Geraldine Jewsbury. Oxford: Oxford University Press: vii–xxv.

Wolff, Robert Lee, 1977. *Gains and Losses: Novels of Faith and Doubt in Victorian England*. London: Murray; New York: Garland Publishing.

Wollstonecraft, Mary, 1792 [1967]. *A Vindication of the Rights of Woman: With Strictures on Political and Moral Subjects*. New York: W. W. Norton & Company, Inc.

Woolf, Virginia, 1932. "Geraldine and Jane", *The Common Reader*, Second Series.

Project Gutenberg. Accessed: 21 January 2017.

___, 1942. "Professions for Women", *The Death of the Moth, and Other Essays*. Project Gutenberg. Accessed: 18 March 2018.

"*Zoe* by Geraldine Jewsbury", Review, *The Critic* (1 February 1845): 313. British Periodicals. Accessed: 1 March 2018.

"*Zoe: The History of Two Lives* by Geraldine Jewsbury", Review, *Literary Gazette and Journal of the Belles Lettres, Arts, Sciences, &c.* 1464 (8 February 1845): 81. British Periodicals. Accessed: 1 March 2018.

Index

Angel in the House, 22, 106, 169–71
Angelo, or the Pine Forest in the Alps, 73–74
Athenaeum, 113–37

Bentley and Son, 139–63
Braddon, Mary Elizabeth, 123, 157–58
Broughton, Rhoda, 9, 125–26, 158–60

Carlyle, Jane Welsh, 8, 30–31, 37–41, 46–54, 57–58, 64, 68, 70, 90–97
Carlyle, Thomas, 8, 32–41, 45, 103
Constance Herbert, 74–75

Dickens, Charles, 79

Eden, Emily, 148–49
education, 4, 62–64, 130–32
Eliot, George, 118–20, 124
Ellis, Sarah Stickney, 70, 126–27

feminism, 1–7, 16–17, 23, 86, 92, 96–97, 113–15, 127–32, 137, 168–69

Gaskell, Elizabeth, 122
genius, 38–39, 63–64, 82–83, 173–74 n. 6

The Half Sisters, 63–68, 162, 173 n. 3

Herschel, Caroline, 135–37
The History of an Adopted Child, 71–73, 75, 77
"How Agnes Worral Was Taught to Be Respectable", 59–60
Household Words, 79–80
Howe, Susanne, 10–11, 168, 170

Ireland, Mrs. Alexander, 9, 91

Jewsbury, Maria Jane, 20–32, 173 n. 2
Johnes, Betha, 106–09

lesbianism, 91–92, 175 n. 4
"The Lower Orders", 59

Mantell, Walter, 6–7, 97–106
Maori, 98, 101
Marian Withers, 68–71
marriage, 5–6, 29, 36, 43, 59–60, 62–63, 72, 82, 103–05, 129–30
Married Women's Property Act, 5–6
Marryat, Florence, 124–25, 152–53
Martin, Lady (Helena Saville Faucit), 109–10
Morgan, Lady (Sydney Owenson), 133–35, 141
Mudie's Circulating Library, 122, 145, 155

Oliphant, Margaret, 147

Ouida, 122–23, 160–61

Paulet, Elizabeth, 46–47, 174 n. 2

religion, 31–35, 44–45, 48–51, 56
Right or Wrong, 77–78

Sand, George, 38–39, 70, 156
sensation novels, 74, 125–26, 155–56
"Social Barbarisms", 58–59
The Sorrows of Gentility, 75–77, 78
"The Story of Angelique", 80–81

Thackeray, William Makepeace, 120, 121
"To-Day", 58
Trollope, Anthony, 120–21

Victoria Regia, 81–82

Woman Question, 114, 127–32
Wood, Mrs. Henry (Ellen), 156–57
Woolf, Virginia, 93, 169–70

Zoe, 43–58

www.ingramcontent.com/pod-product-compliance
Lightning Source LLC
Chambersburg PA
CBHW060953230426
43665CB00015B/2183